The Persistence of Gender Inequality

The Persistence of Gender Inequality

Mary Evans

polity

First published in 2017 by Polity Press

Polity Press
65 Bridge Street
Cambridge CB2 1UR, UK

Polity Press
350 Main Street
Malden, MA 02148, USA

ISBN-13: 978-0-7456-8991-3
ISBN-13: 978-0-7456-8992-0(pb)

A catalogue record for this book is available from the British Library.

Library of Congress Cataloging-in-Publication Data

Names: Evans, Mary, 1946- author.
Title: The persistence of gender inequality / Mary Evans.
Description: Cambridge, UK ; Malden, MA : Polity Press, 2016. | Includes
    bibliographical references and index.
Identifiers: LCCN 2016017192 (print) | LCCN 2016028399 (ebook) | ISBN
    9780745689913 (hardcover : alk. paper) | ISBN 0745689914 (hardcover : alk.
    paper) | ISBN 9780745689920 (pbk. : alk. paper) | ISBN 0745689922 (pbk. :
    alk. paper) | ISBN 9780745689944 (mobi) | ISBN 9780745689951 (epub)
Subjects: LCSH: Sex discrimination. | Women's rights. | Equality. | Sex role.
Classification: LCC HQ1237 .E9175 2016 (print) | LCC HQ1237 (ebook) | DDC
    305.3--dc23
LC record available at https://lccn.loc.gov/2016017192

Typeset in 10.5 on 12 pt Sabon by Servis Filmsetting Ltd, Stockport, Cheshire
Printed and bound in the UK by Clays Ltd, St Ives PLC

For further information on Polity, visit our website: www.politybooks.com

Contents

Acknowledgements

I have many people to thank for their various forms of help and support. My thanks, therefore to Emma Longstaff, who first suggested that I write this book, and subsequently to Jonathan Skerrett of Polity for all his help and that of the anonymous reviewers of earlier drafts of this book. Fiona Sewell was an exemplary copy editor, whose work here has been invaluable. I should also like to thank everyone, staff and students, at the Gender Institute of the London School of Economics for providing such a supportive and informative context whilst I was writing this book. It has been a privilege and a pleasure to be there.

I want to acknowledge the part that wide-ranging conversations, often about subjects other than this book, have played in enlivening the process of writing it. So my very warm thanks to Rose Abderabbani, Anne Barron, Liz Cocks, Elizabeth Cowie, Marie Corbin, Diane Cunningham, Kathy Davis, Barbara Einhorn, Sarah Evans, John Jervis, Hazel Johnstone, Cadence Kinsey, Sonia Kruks, Jan Montefiore, Janet Sayers, Maggie Schaedel, Jenny Uglow, Clare Ungerson and Anna Witham. Ralph Kinnear gave crucial help with the final stages of the manuscript. My sons Thomas and James have provided an endless source of happiness as well as much-valued forms of assistance.

Preface

This book is written against the backdrop of bitter and devastating conflicts in many parts of the world. In many of those contexts one of the central issues is the appropriate order of relations between men and women. Whilst the social and political rights of women are greater in some places than others, there is no country where gender equality has been achieved. The question of why not, of why change should be so difficult and so challenging, is the subject here. From what Laura Bates has described as 'everyday' sexism to brutally enforced regimes of gender differentiation, biological difference continues to bring with it distinct, and often radically distinct, implications.[1] Addressing this reality and the part that it continues to play in global politics is the subject here. Not least in the discussion is the issue of who profits from gendered inequality.

Questions about the relationship between women and men have a long lineage, and this book does not intend to review that long history or the academic work about it. This book is essentially about the present, about what is called, variously, late capitalism, neoliberalism or late modernity. There is considerable distance between these titles but all relate to the world of the twentieth and twenty-first centuries. It is commonly assumed that connections and relationships between parts of this world are closer than ever before. In this, what is also often assumed – and it will be a central issue discussed here – is that the lives of men and women are becoming more similar, and that distinctions made on the basis of biology are disappearing. What continues is that men and women share, as they have always done, the immediate circumstance of their lives, and for many people alive today that circumstance is the political economy of capitalism; not the form known to historians of the eighteenth or nineteenth century but the form about which Beatrix Campbell has written '[this] new articulation of capitalism and patriarchy is hegemonic. That does not make it stable: all over the world there is tumult and resistance.'[2]

The tumult and resistance of which Campbell writes have various forms, from those not specifically focused on gender politics, such as the 'Arab Spring' or the protests of the Occupy movement in the United States, to those much more explicitly about gender, such as protests about sexual violence against women, internet sexism or punitive attacks on homosexuality. Globally, however, what is clear is that the politics of gender are part of what the sociologists Luc Boltanski and Eve Chiapello have described as the 'new spirit of capitalism', a form which has produced a curious paradox: that of the increasing instability and uncertainty of material existence accompanied by an abandonment of previous forms of the control of individual choices, notably that of sexuality.[3] In the UK, for example, the years 2010–15 have seen a determined assault on all forms of state provision whilst a 'new Conservatism' allows diverse forms of sexual relationships, for example that of same-sex marriage. In this context, what will be explored in the following pages are the complexities of not only the continuity of gender inequality but also its constant reappearance in new forms. In particular, what will be suggested is that whilst millions of women, by virtue of their biological association with care, are widely exploited, the fantasies and ideals of femininity constitute the basis of exploitative and highly profitable forms of consumption.

These two aspects of the exploitation of women and the feminine are found in the context of a growing social inequality that besets the lives of men and women throughout the world. The optimism of previous decades, in which the goal of the elimination of poverty was the aspiration of many countries, has been replaced by more pessimistic expectations in which it is assumed that the majority will not see rising standards of living. But the politics necessary to contest this has to recognize more specific forms of inequality than that of overall social inequality, forms which do not just produce different aspects of inequality but contribute to and help to maintain overall social inequality. The persistence of gender inequality is not, therefore, only about the specific inequalities and injustices experienced by women but about the ways in which those conditions help to maintain general, structural and increasingly considerable forms of inequality. The aim here is to explore the part that the various forms, processes and contexts of gender differentiation play in maintaining a wider order of social inequality.

1

What is Gender Inequality?

Debates about gender have existed in both print and daily life for generations, and heated discussions about the state of relations between men and women show little sign of decreasing. In the early decades of the twenty-first century, issues about gender and sexual identity have become the subjects of increasingly complex debates, whilst the actual lived experience of gender can still be defined by rigid and often non-negotiable assumptions derived from biological difference. For example, debates arising out of the politics of transgender have called into question the very meaning of the terms 'male' and 'female,' whilst in certain parts of the world these very definitions of identity constitute mandatory forms of social existence. Discussions about gender exist universally; it is the nature of the debate, and certainly the degree to which it is a matter of public debate, that differ. But apart from these debates – about the implications of biological difference – there is a considerable degree of consensus that women, both born and made, have less access to power and privilege than men. Hence, although we speak of 'gender inequality', the term here has a more specific focus. It refers to those various social inequalities which are more often experienced by women than men. Those inequalities take forms which will be the basis of the discussion here and in later chapters: those of material and political disadvantage and of various forms of abusive representation.

At that point, and through the use of the apparently inclusive term 'women', we encounter a potential minefield: a minefield in which much of the strength of that binary division between women and men is disrupted. Questions of class, of race, of sexual identity, of age, of ethnicity all disrupt any simplistic view that gender 'inequality' is solely a question of all men having more power and privilege than all women. There are two reasons for this: one is the point that the American academic Kimberlé Cranshaw made in 1991 when she wrote about the 'multiple grounds of identity' – of gender, race and class - which we all occupy. In doing so she articulated the concept of 'intersectionality', the recognition that all human beings are located within conditions of class and race as well as that of gender.[1] The second reason is that the terms power and privilege are no less problematic. In the second decade of the twenty-first century it is becoming demonstrably clear that power and privilege, in terms of access to material resources and control over the lives of others, are not just as concentrated as they have been in the past but are becoming both increasingly so and at the same time distant from any form of public, democratic scrutiny. The vast majority of men and women are, in this context, united by living outside that tiny minority where wealth and power are situated.

Yet amongst that majority of the world's population which lives outside the world of substantial wealth there are important differences which divide us. Many of those differences have until recently been expressed in a distinction between the 'global north' and the 'global south'. This division – between worlds of material plenty and worlds of material poverty – has lost some of its resonance as we have come to recognize that these categories have less homogeneity than has been supposed, and that neither poverty nor wealth is exclusively the preserve of particular geographical areas.[2] This is not to evade or obscure the very real differences that exist in the lives of the world's population, but it is to recognize that one of those straightforward divisions between 'the west' and the other parts of the world has often been supported by comparisons between the situation of women in the industrialized world and elsewhere. In this, what has been assumed is a distinction between the 'emancipation' of women in the 'modern' west and the lack of emancipation in other parts of the world. It is an assumption that has played its part in the global politics of the legitimization of militarized engagements. For example, taking 'emancipation' to the women of Afghanistan was presented as part of the justification of the twenty-first-century military campaign led by the United States and the United Kingdom against the Taliban. Largely ignored was what was described in 1984 by Edward Said as the problem of 'travelling theory', the western practice of imposing on other countries its templates for social existence, not the least of which was the asymmetry between the dominant and the subject races.[3] In this instance, the introduction of a legal framework for gender equality did not (in Afghanistan as elsewhere) immediately produce that reality. The assumptions, habits and culture of patriarchy, as women throughout the global north have discovered, do not automatically disappear with changes in the law or other forms of institutional rearrangement.

The part that ambitions about progress towards greater equality between men and women can play in legitimizations of western military interventions is an important instance of a widespread contemporary view about gender relations, namely that there was a steady progress towards equality in the twentieth-century west. It is an assumption which has appeared in various forms, perhaps most vividly in the infamous slogan used in a cigarette advertisement campaign in 1968: 'You've come a long way, baby'. What this campaign did was to position an account of the past (for example, in one advertisement, the statement that 'In the past a man allowed his wife one day a week out of the house') against what was suggested as contemporary reality. The fictional man and the equally fictional woman of the present day (who could still be addressed by advertisers as 'baby') were presented as equally independent, urban, young, white and autonomous. The 'new' woman of the latter part of the twentieth century was the woman who took a full part in what was assumed to be the norm of modern existence. That life was one of paid work, financial independence and sexual choice. In these contexts, it was assumed, gender equality had been achieved. But perhaps most important about this advertisement was the way in which the very judgement about women, and their changed status, came from a masculinized voice. It was not women who were naming their own situation; it was being defined by men.

This book does not reject the view that there have been important changes in the lives of women and men in the past one hundred years. But what it does reject is the idea that these changes can easily be assumed as 'progress' and that equality between men and women now exists. Thus, although important alterations have taken place throughout the world in the legal status of women and men, many of the various contexts within which we 'do' gender changed remarkably little in the twentieth or the first decades of the twenty-first centuries. Perhaps most centrally what has not changed is the relationship of women to the work of care. That category involves not just the sometimes recognized (if not rewarded) work of the care of dependents but the more subtle assumption that part of the social meaning of womanhood is that of the caring human. The associative strength of this connection has endured for centuries. It remains intact and as such is responsible for much of the radically unequal way in which all women (with or without dependents) exist within the world of paid work. But this world is increasingly precarious and socially divided. The place of women in this context is structured through not only the habits of the past but also the specific inequalities of the present.

Amongst these inequalities are those which, as suggested, unite rather than divide women and men. For example, the British geographer Danny Dorling writes of the growing disparity between 'the rich' and 'the rest' in terms of the dramatic slogan, echoed in the rhetoric of the Anglo-American Occupy movement, of the '1%'.[4] In this there are no distinctions of gender. This is important to notice, not just because of the absence of a gendered analysis, but because no discussion about gender inequality can ignore or overlook other forms of inequality. Hence the question of gender inequality has to be seen not in terms of static and idealized forms of achieving 'equality' but in terms of the ever-changing and evolving meaning and reality of overall social inequality. The comfortable – although mistaken – assumption of the achievement of gender equality leaves unanswered questions, for example, about the way in which the global pay gap between women and men contributes to the accumulation of that wealth which is constitutive of patterns of growing social inequality.

Making Inequality

The view that we should be highly sceptical about the achievement of gender equality has become more generally current for two reasons. The first is that it has become increasingly apparent throughout the world that new media of communication provide a form through which women, both generally and specifically, can be threatened and derided. High-profile cases of these kinds of instances have been the internet attacks on (amongst others in the UK) the academic Mary Beard and the campaigner Caroline Criado-Perez. Mary Beard had challenged the attacks on women who voiced political opinions; Caroline Priado-Perez had suggested that Jane Austen might appear on UK banknotes. The second reason is that the austerity politics that have become common throughout much of Europe since 2010 have impacted in especially damaging ways on women; Ruth Pearson and Diane Elson are amongst those who have set out particularly clearly the impact of financial austerity on women.[5] Others, such as Linda Tirado for the United States and Lisa McKenzie for the UK, have discussed more general aspects of austerity's impact.[6] In these two circumstances women have raised questions about the forms of inequality which women globally encounter. Jacqueline Rose, for example, in her 2014 book *Women in Dark Times*, wrote that 'Women are not free today – not even in the West, where the inequalities are still glaring.'[7] A central thesis here, shared by Rose and other writers such as Laurie Penny and Laura Bates and by groups in the UK such as the Women's Budget Group, is that we live in what has been described (in the words of Rose) as both a time of 'unprecedented violence against women' and one where new conditions of paid work and 'austerity' politics have been damaging to millions of women.[8] These neoliberal policies have not of themselves created material poverty amongst women – women's average pay has always been lower than that of men, and women have consistently been a marginal presence in public politics – but they have enlarged the contours of gendered inequality through, amongst other policies, the decrease in jobs traditionally taken by women in the public sector and in those services (such as forms of publicly provided care) that are central to women's lives.

In recognizing the ways in which neoliberal policies have had specific, and negative, consequences for women, there also has to be an engagement with the implications of political narratives which assume that change is always positive and that the changes instituted in what we think of as the 'modern' world are always for the better. One of the aspects of this view is particularly important here: the belief that to 'modernize' is to extend the boundaries of human freedom, to shake off the strictures and the confines of the past and bring into being a 'new' society. Political rhetoric, particularly in the west, is markedly enthusiastic about 'modernization' without much consideration of either its meaning or its possible consequences. This vagueness about the term 'modernization' has allowed, since the early 2000s, neoliberal policies to be presented as forms of 'modernization', regardless of their socially regressive consequences.

It is the generally socially regressive consequences of neoliberal policies that have been the focus of other widely influential forms of critique. The works of authors such as Joseph Stiglitz, Anthony Atkinson, Thomas Piketty, Danny Dorling, Ha-Joon Chang, Kate Pickett and Richard Wilkinson have formed powerful – although often theoretically distinct – accounts of general social inequality, which exist parallel to accounts of the specific inequality of women.[9] The question here, however, is that whilst the publications of this group of authors (and others with similar views) are important, and a daily rebuttal to neoliberal narratives about the merits of largely unregulated markets and a smaller state, it is work, as its various critics have pointed out, in which the implications of the socially inscribed differences of gender play little part.[10] Amongst those absences, which have nevertheless been a longstanding presence in feminist economics, is the discussion of the impact of women's unpaid work on that of paid work.[11] For generations, the care work (paid and unpaid) of women has been read consistently by mainstream economists as of little value. It is not that individuals have not venerated and welcomed care, but that both market and state socialist economies have had no place in their political understanding for what constitutes the social value of care work. There is a longstanding assumption that the work of what is sometimes known as social reproduction is essentially that of inferior people. Here is Adam Smith, writing in 1776 in *The Wealth of Nations* that 'The Labour of a menial servant . . . adds to the value of nothing.'[12] We might view this comment as the dismissal by a privileged white male of those who supported his everyday life – and Katrine Marcal has raised the question of who cooked Adam Smith's dinner – were it not for the comments made in the twentieth century by (it has to be said) equally privileged white women.[13] Thus Simone de Beauvoir wrote, in 1949 in *The Second Sex*, about the futility and the repetition of housework; human dependence on others has little presence in the book.[14] As negative as these views are about the centrality to human existence of the work of social reproduction and the social relationships that it involves, they are fleeting when compared to the views expressed about different kinds of work by Hannah Arendt in *The Human Condition*, first published in 1958. In this book, Arendt outlined her account of the three possible forms of human existence: labour, work and action. What is striking about this trio of possibilities is less the importance placed on work and action than the radical unimportance of what Arendt defines as labour. For Arendt this is the form of work which involves the reproduction and continuation of daily life, the work historically performed either by slaves or by servants. In this context, Arendt writes, we find no real equality but only debasement.

The views of Arendt and Beauvoir are suggestive of global traditions which assign neither status nor significant reward to what is variously described as care work, social reproduction or housework. This is a position from which the emancipation of women is seen to lie firmly in the rejection of any form of association with traditional forms of femininity and in an identification with what is construed as the world of men. A challenge to the assumed irrelevance of this care work to ongoing human existence came from feminist campaigns in the 1970s which achieved some political presence for this work through its formal and monetary recognition of it. But the problematic relationship between gender and the public and private worlds remains. In this, the global north assumes that the public world – of paid work and engagement with various institutional and creative worlds – is increasingly one which is open to all, on similar terms. That this is both true and untrue is part of our recent history, in which the UK has had a woman prime minister, and, at the time of writing this, it is possible that the USA might have a woman president. But in those examples, residual ideas about the meaning of femininity are apparent.

When her husband was running for election as president of the United States, Hillary Clinton had to prove her association with, and sympathy for, housewifely skills by providing recipes for biscuits. On the other side of the Atlantic Margaret Thatcher consistently made much of her involvement in the running of her household. She also brought to the discussion of public finances comments drawn from the management of domestic budgets, a way of thinking about economic policy which has remained, with all its many limitations, to this day. These were curious and contradictory examples of the power of the ancient connection between women and the home. The past might be a different place, but in the case of public attitudes to women, the gendered connections between paid work and public presence are clearly still with us. What we are presented with is a powerful western tradition which assigns little public or symbolic importance to domestic work and an equally powerful tradition which demands that women continue to perform it.

The emphasis on the social location of women within the private space of the household – and responsibility for it – flies in the face of evidence from across centuries and locations that significant numbers of women have always been in paid work. In the UK, for example, the 1851 Census (the first of its kind in Britain) recorded that 40 per cent of adult women were in some form of financially rewarding labour. This fact, the contemporary form of which is now read through narratives of 'modernization' as a form of women's emancipation, had as much to do then as it has now with material reality. The rise in the cost of living (particularly, in some areas of some countries, of the cost of housing) has made paid work essential for the majority of adults. The 'other duties' of mothers which William Beveridge argued would (and implicitly should) keep them out of paid work exist as much in the second decade of the twenty-first century as they did in 1942 when Beveridge was writing the blueprint of the British welfare state. However, those 'other duties' of care coexist with that financial imperative of paid work, which takes place in those increasingly precarious ways which Beatrix Campbell and others have recorded. At the same time, just as many states have diminished (or never had) welfare provision, those same states have now also increased the energy with which state-provided benefits are policed. In this context, that of precarious employment and increasingly limited forms of state support, women have been radically disadvantaged by that very dynamic of social 'change', namely the greater numbers of women in paid employment, which has been read as an inevitably emancipatory form. It is also the case that women, again as ever, have provided a rich source for moralizing accounts of the 'good' and the 'bad' poor. From the careless mothers of William Hogarth's eighteenth-century 'Gin Lane', to the 'feckless' mothers of the nineteenth and twentieth centuries and the benefits 'cheats' of the twenty-first, women have been targets for politically charged abuse.

From this what might follow is a narrative of miserabilism – not the conventional form which sees all change as change for the worse – but rather a form of miserabilism which assumes that 'some things' will always stay the same, that they are ordered in certain 'natural' ways and that radical change only ever has negative consequences. That reading of the dynamic of social life is not part of this account of gender inequality, but it does raise the question of ambiguous meanings and implications of the word 'change'. 'Change' is deemed in some ways an essential component of what is taken for granted as the proper progress of a 'modern' society, and yet in others an often unwelcome form of novel events or social relations. For some the idea of 'change' is part and parcel of what is also commonly vindicated as 'growth'; the idea that if a society fails to continue to 'modernize' and enlarge its productive capacity it will stagnate. Collectively, the words 'change', 'modernization' and 'progress' might well be regarded as 'weasel' words,

words that inform and define with little considered sense of their meaning. Gender relations take place within this vocabulary: the assertion of gender equality and the emancipation of women are part of the way in which our self-perception as 'modern' is vindicated. We congratulate ourselves that our 'modern' society is not to be confused with those societies and cultures where contemporary gender relations are often described in terms of the historical past, a past from which our capacity to change has freed us.

What Has Changed?

What occurs through this appetite for self-congratulation is twofold: it fails to recognize the various reasons why gender relations have changed and, just as importantly, why they have not changed. We cannot fail to notice, for example, that parents have fewer children than was the case at the beginning of the twentieth century. Nor can we fail to notice that our definition of 'parents' has widened to include parents of the same sex. But at the same time, it remains women who perform most of the care of those children. Equally, whilst the visible face of public power has included more women, what might be termed the 'private' face of power (the institutional power, state and corporate, that defines and supports many of the circumstances in which public power operates) remains overwhelmingly male. It is only necessary to read the footnotes of the two volumes of Charles Moore's biography of Margaret Thatcher to see revealed the very white, male, public-school and Oxbridge-educated make-up of the British political class.[15] Despite these factors an ongoing narrative suggests, from various political perspectives, that gender equality has been achieved. This fiction about the world is then continued in a variety of forms. From socially conservative readings of history comes the idea that women have taken over the world and/or that men are now the victims of the empowerment of women. These various forms of fantasy are of course in part an expression of our ceaseless appetite for sensation and sensational headlines in which, for example, women who have drunk too much become headline news and apparently indicative of general changes in the behaviour of women. This kind of instance will reliably attract viewers and readers even if an examination of these headlines demonstrates the complete absence of evidence about the phenomenon that is being presented as 'fact'.

On another part of the political spectrum, left-wing accounts of the recent history of the west, like those of the Marxist historian Eric Hobsbawm, argue that the change in the social situation of women is the most fundamental social change of the twentieth century.[16] Others from different parts of the political spectrum have expressed the same view. But this view – whilst entirely credible in the way that women, like men, have benefitted from many forms of technological change and universal improvements in education and health care – is challenged here for three reasons. First, 'austerity' demonstrates how considerable remains the reliance of women on the state for material and legal forms of support to make good the structural disadvantages of being female. The refuges for women subject to domestic violence and the access to respite for many carers are just two examples of socially essential services that have been put at risk by 'austerity' politics in the UK. Second, new forms of gender inequality are emerging in, as already suggested, new media of communication which make possible abusive attacks on women; and third, many of the privileges enjoyed by women in the global north are dependent either very specifically, in terms of individualized forms of help, or through more distant forms of connection on the exploitation of women (and men) in the global south. Thus gendered inequality is being considered here through those three forms of inequality, all of which are connected and all of which work, in different ways, to the collective advantage both of individual men and, most importantly, of a small group of very wealthy individuals, both male and female. The advantages to individual men of gendered inequality may be limited and even amenable to personal negotiation and change; the advantages to a wealthy class are structural and beyond the control of any one individual.

Changing Conditions

But challenges to various forms of gendered power are not absent. Individual situations can offer interpersonal gender equality, and on certain occasions (and policies in the UK and the USA during the two world wars were significant instances of this) wider social circumstances have forced governments to implement policies involving women that might otherwise have been resisted. At all times, too, what is crucial to recall is that the everyday facts of material existence have propelled women into seeking changes in their circumstances. Strikes by women in Britain and the United States in the later decades of the nineteenth century and the early years of the twentieth century (most famously the strike at the Bryant and May match factory in London in 1888 and the 'Uprising of the 20,000' in New York in 1903) brought together women in forms of collective action that were at least as significant as that of the suffrage campaigns. The continuation of the ways in which women's paid labour was consistently undervalued was similarly central in the later years of the twentieth century in the strikes in the UK at both the Ford factory at Dagenham in 1968 and Grunwick in 1976-8. Both are testament to the situations in which immediate forms of social reality have encouraged women to demand change.[17] Yet it is misleading to suppose that there was any inevitable connection between male, solidaristic labour organizations and the cause of women workers in seeking changes, for example, during the Grunwick strike. As Jayaben Desai, one of the leaders of that strike, said of the Trades Union Congress, 'Trade Union support is like honey on the elbow – you can smell it, you can feel it, but you cannot taste it.'[18]

The Grunwick strike, together with others in both the UK and the USA, also suggest that it is important to question a too straightforward and causal relationship between the written history of western feminism and the emergence of specific feminist campaigns. The written history of feminism is usually dated as beginning in the late eighteenth century, with Mary Wollstonecraft's 1792 *A Vindication of the Rights of Woman*, and proceeding along a path that leads via Simone de Beauvoir's *The Second Sex* to the many works of feminists in the 1970s and beyond. But the use of a chronological narrative here can obscure the complex links between different forms and generations of feminism and their contextual situations. For example, it is important to stress the ways in which many of the demands made by white feminists on both sides of the Atlantic in the nineteenth century were for access to the same forms of privilege as men, and that feminism – as the divisions within the Pankhurst family between the socialist Sylvia and her more conservative mother Emmeline demonstrated – did not always produce consistent political agreement between women. The one aspect that did remain consistent from the eighteenth century onwards was the demand by women for an education similar to that allowed to men. Decades before Mary Wollstonecraft wrote her famous appeal for the better education of women, Mary Astell had voiced, in 1694, a similar idea; both demand an education that is equal to that of men, and in doing so establish that emphasis on education that has been such a continuing theme in liberal feminism. Mary Astell wrote – in words which remain relevant in terms of today's celebrity culture – 'Let us learn to pride ourselves in something more excellent than the invention of a fashion.'[19] As the scope and social meaning of 'education' changed, so agitation for the access of women to universities and professional training was a characteristic of much of the global north in the nineteenth century, even though definitions of both education and class are sometimes surprising to readers in the twenty-first century. For example, those running the British Female Middle Class Emigration Society in the mid-nineteenth century defined 'middle class' in terms of the possession of skills in cooking, washing, needlework and baking: skills which would seldom be listed in our contemporary understanding of either middle class or emancipation.[20] What is so remarkable about these – and other – nineteenth- and early twentieth-century documents of women's history is the assumption, across lines of class and race, that the primary skill that women should possess is the ability to run a stable and ordered household. There are certainly nineteenth-century societies actively campaigning for access to universities, the vote and access to the professions, but the ethos of what was enshrined in a poem by Coventry Patmore in 1854 of woman as the 'angel in the house' was very powerful and wide-ranging, as too has been the emphasis on the 'respectability' of the women in various campaigns across time and place.[21]

This emphasis on 'respectability' found a secure home in many of the feminist campaigns of the early twentieth century in Britain and the United States. In both countries much was made (and had been made since the time of Mary Wollstonecraft) of the altruistic motive of aspects of feminism: that educating women would make a better life for both individuals and society. More disruptive figures – in continental Europe, Alexandra Kollontai and Rosa Luxemburg – were rather less concerned with making a better form of existing society and rather more with radical transformation. Similarly awkward questions about the relationship of feminism to other politics were asked by Emma Goldman, whose work and political engagement straddled continents. She was to write, at the beginning of the twentieth century, that 'The movement for women's emancipation has so far made but the first step in that direction.'[22] But it is also appropriate to recall here that one of British literary modernism's most influential writers, Virginia Woolf, became equally sceptical of what she saw as both reformist feminism and its relationship to any lasting transformation of gender relations. Thus from those early decades of the twentieth century, in which many countries began to embrace a self-conscious sense of themselves as 'modern' nation states, Woolf asked awkward questions about feminism. Her *Three Guineas* of 1938 argued less for what might be described as reform and much more for the possibilities of radical disorder. Writing about Woolf's essay, her biographer Hermione Lee commented that 'The essay was a threat . . . furious, lacerating, harsh and awkward.'[23] It was not just that Woolf attacked key social institutions; she pilloried the very mindsets that made them possible. In doing so, she established a distance, both for herself and for subsequent generations between those who see feminism in terms of demands for access to privileged forms of power and those who wish to rethink the very existence of those sites of power. 'Speaking truth to power' did not, Woolf reminds us, necessarily involve asking for greater access to it.

The institutions which Woolf challenged (the universities, the Church of England, the military, the judiciary) persist today, in similar forms across the world. Even though all of them, with different degrees of the absence of enthusiasm, have allowed women access to their lofty portals, they retain that characteristic which Woolf recognized almost a hundred years ago: a determination to maintain their own power and the social relations that are implicit in that power. The difference is that women have now been, at least formally, allowed to share in aspects of that power; the question of the extent to which those institutions have been transformed by the presence of women (however marginal that presence may be at a senior level) is one that remains contentious. Yet that question has important political implications, since it raises issues about essentialist assumptions of different male and female qualities, as well as often taking for granted the many forms of hierarchy and difference that powerful institutions adopt and support. So whilst the proportion of women in various powerful institutions (most notably those related to religion, the military and finance) has increased very little since 1938, what have changed are aspects of the cultural world in which those institutions are grounded. Notably, there is a greater expectation of the public toleration of the sexual choices and identities of its citizens. This expectation is far from generally fulfilled, and it is apparent that all kinds of attacks – from verbal bullying to physical assault – are still part of the lives of too many citizens whose sexual identities diverge from the norms of heterosexuality. Nevertheless, Jeffrey Weeks is correct to write, in *The World We Have Won*, that much of the general culture of the global north is more tolerant of openly expressed sexual diversity than it once was. But, as studies of lived experience within hierarchical and powerful institutions demonstrate, whilst aspects of the wider culture may have changed, the internal lives of powerful institutions have not necessarily been so receptive. In her important study of gender and the City of London, Linda McDowell has noted the greater appreciation of 'feminine' qualities in men, but rather less enthusiasm for 'masculine' qualities in women.[24] In the United States, research by Kristen Schilt has suggested that women who transgender to male increase their earning power and status within corporate hierarchies.[25] What this suggests is that the (largely male) human beings who 'do' power may sanction forms of greater sexual diversity but in practice keep the expectations and assumptions that maintain gender inequality.

So whilst we might look back at the twentieth century and see how some forms of social power have shifted, and in particular see the emergence of public discourses about sexuality which make it easier for both women and men to live public sexual lives of their own choosing, we have also to consider what has remained consistent, as well as the question of how change is produced. 'Doing' and living gender in the early twenty-first century allows many citizens of the west greater diversity of sexual choice and less obedience to what Adrienne Rich memorably called 'compulsory heterosexuality'.[26] But in the second decade of the twenty-first century, as much as in the third decade of the twentieth when *Three Guineas* was published, all citizens, apart from a very small minority (the infamous '1%' of political slogans), depend upon earned income in order to support themselves, and they do so in worlds variously described as market economies, or capitalism, or – with more rhetorical force if less accuracy - the 'free' world. The rewards for work to meet that fundamental need to provide for oneself and/or others are consistently different across divisions of class, race and gender, and have provided occupation for generations of specialists as well as intense political disagreement. Those various inequalities within the material conditions and relationships in which we 'do' gender have changed remarkably little in the past century; indeed, much social research suggests that, in the UK and the United States in particular, social inequality is actually increasing, with little or no improvement in the social expectations of significant groups – in the United States Afro-Americans, in Britain the white working class.[27] Here it is appropriate to mention just one aspect of ongoing discussions about gendered disparities of power and wealth.

The aspect in question is that men continue to dominate hierarchies of public, institutional power. However frequently examples of individual women who have attained public office are cited, they cannot negate the extent of the absence of women from these positions. Whether or not, and how, the presence of women would transform these hierarchies is at least as important a question: some evidence from Scandinavian countries suggests that a higher proportion of women in national politics can alter the focus and emphasis of public policy, most notably making it more concerned with general questions of responsibility for the care of others.[28] But this shift in what are, fundamentally, arrangements of the welfare arm of the capitalist state does not appear to be accompanied by a shift in other aspects of national politics, most notably that of a political affiliation to the values of a market economy, in particular those of individual competition and a very limited public sector. Those values became especially apparent during the period when Margaret Thatcher was prime minister of the UK and Ronald Reagan was president of the USA. In both countries there was a determined attack on the post-Second World War consensus about the role of the state in providing both public services and public investment. The 'neocons', as the ideologues and politicians of neoliberalism have been described, espoused the ideals of what Daniel Stedman Jones has described as 'free market individualism'. Moreover, these views, Stedman Jones suggests, affect not just two countries but the entire planet: 'The neoliberal vision of globalization was that a system based on individual freedom, free markets, and the opportunities provided by "flexible labor markets" would substitute for universal high-quality publicly funded education and health care systems, more efficient and cheaper privatised alternatives. The citizen was nothing more than a consumer.'[29] Stedman Jones's consumer is gender neutral, a neutrality which – like the gender neutral citizen of Piketty et al. – obscures aspects of gender inequality, not least of the responsibilities of life outside paid work.

There are four aspects of this generalization about the neoliberal subject which are important here. The first is that neoliberal economic and social policies have produced conditions which have eroded any possible absence from paid work for the majority of adults. Paradoxically, an inherently conservative ideology, more usually associated with the view that women's place is in the home, has produced what has long been assumed to be the basis of the emancipation of women: participation in paid work. Women, whilst remaining the caring subject of public and political expectation, have also become an employed subject and subsumed into the rhetoric of the 'hard-working' person. But entering this increasingly competitive and precarious context of paid work has only been achieved for many women on terms which reflect ancient values about the work which women do. So women come to the workforce with an identity formed through expectations about their role as carers. In much of the paid work of care (or catering or cleaning) in which women are employed, they then encounter the double negative of being women in women's work.

The second issue which is important here, and which bears on the question of the relationship between gendered and social inequality, is that of the intensification of credentialism. As we have seen, feminists have for centuries held as central aims the greater access of women to higher education and the professions. In the global north this has largely been achieved. But against that, the increased segmentation of higher education across the west has had the negative effect of entrenching differences of class and race and maintaining classed and racialized differences between women. In 2015 the British sociologist Mike Savage published a study of class in England in which he wrote:

> Entry to the most privileged careers is more and more demanding, depending not only on access to elite universities but to an intense portfolio of internships, social networking and cultural activity . . . Given the widening distance (economically, socially and geographically) between the super-rich and the rest of us . . . the 21st century is likely to be marked by increasingly disruptive challenges to the social fabric. The old class war may be over: the new politics of class is only just beginning.[30]

Savage, like other writers on social inequality in the twenty-first century, does not focus on gendered inequality. But – again in common with others – his work is nevertheless important here, because through the study of class inequality it can bring to the study of gender inequality both a recognition of its classed forms and a way of considering how gendered relations to power and privilege are reproduced. For instance, that 'demanding' entry to the more elite professions of which Savage writes has traditionally been secured through endorsed forms of masculinity. How those forms might be represented by women remains problematic and relates to the longstanding issue within feminism of its uneasy and unresolved relationship to social divisions other than that of gender. Those divisions have been consistently disturbing; the British historian Barbara Taylor remarked of feminism in the late twentieth century that 'there were too many inequalities among us – of class, ethnicity, cultural advantages, financial resources – for a lasting solidarity'.[31]

These comments echo those of Mike Savage about the processes of division, selection and exclusion that characterize social structures not just in Britain but throughout the world. Yet in the face of persisting divisions there are – and have been for centuries – calls for unity between women across boundaries of class and race. This takes us to a third issue about gendered inequality in the twenty-first century: the potential unity of women. Given what has been said so far about classed and racialized inequality in the global north, and what could also be said (and will be said at greater length in the following chapter) about gendered forms of inequality between the global north and the global south, the extent of this unity might appear limited. So whilst there is an increasing acceptance that the refusal to extend the full rights of citizenship to all women becomes ever more bizarre, if not perverse, as the twenty-first century continues, the use of the word 'women' as a unifying political term raises problems. It does this less because of the important ways in which the word retains its collective force than because of the ways in which it has sometimes been used, with few qualifications of the differences between women, to discuss contexts which are radically socially unequal. An example of this is the call by Sheryl Sandberg, the chief operating officer of Facebook, for women to 'lean in', to demand a greater share of corporate power.[32] Now the subject of discussion by many on the web, as well as in *Lean Out* by Dawn Foster, Sandberg's book calls on women to revive that Dickensian move of 'asking for more'.[33] Whether or not individual women will have more success than Oliver Twist remains to be seen.

Sandberg's definition of a truly equal world as 'one where women ran half our countries and companies and men ran half our homes' does little to confront the impact of social and gender inequality. In many ways she has assumed, as Alison Wolf did in her book *The XX Factor: How Working Women Are Creating a New*

Society, that ever-greater demands from material circumstances on both women and men will somehow create greater gender equality, or that, as Hanna Rosin has suggested, men will somehow disappear from senior positions in the workforce.[34] Even though Sandberg writes that she is 'acutely aware that the vast majority of women are struggling to make ends meet and take care of their families', this qualification is never, as is often the case, thought through in terms of exactly *why* so many women are 'struggling' and what powerful corporations might have to do with this.[35] The 'struggle' to which Sandberg refers might also be considered in terms of the multiple demands that 'liquid modernity' (as the sociologist Zygmunt Baumann has described that world of the twenty-first century, in which Facebook plays an active part) makes on women in particular.[36] In this world, new material demands and ever-greater competition for secure forms of employment are less and less mitigated by various forms of state provision or legal protection. The connections between poverty, vulnerability and gender remain just as important and awkward as they were in the past. Sandberg's book (in common with *Unfinished Business* by Anne-Marie Slaughter) vividly – if implicitly – demonstrates the conceptual refusal of the inequalities that exist within neoliberalism.[37]

This also takes us to the fourth and final point here: the ways in which gendered fantasies about the making of a 'good life' in the twentieth and the twenty-first century intersect with those fantasies of femininity, particularly the continuing presence of that domestic spectre of the 'angel in the house', in maintaining and furthering inequalities both social and gendered. To illustrate how this might occur it is useful to turn to twentieth- and twenty-first-century fiction about the horrific possibilities, for both women and men, of living within the domestic, largely suburban, dream in which a woman presides over the world of the nuclear family. For example, Richard Yates, in his 1961 novel *Revolutionary Road*, and Evan S. Connell, in his 1959 novel *Mrs Bridge*, explored, in the years immediately before Betty Friedan's *The Feminine Mystique*, the negative consequences for individuals of the construction of heterosexual relationships around the values, norms and aspirations of private consumption and aspirational personal narratives.

Most dramatically, Sylvia Plath's *The Bell Jar* conveyed a great many of the various anxieties around the maintenance of highly classed and racialized fantasies of the 'good life'.[38] In the twenty-first century a work of detective fiction set against the background of the collapse of the Irish housing market, Tana French's *Broken Harbour*, connected the non-fictional collapse of the Republic of Ireland's housing market with the collapse of domestic dreams.[39] In this novel a woman's ambitions about the making of an 'ideal' family home go tragically wrong. When the dream of life in what is described by the estate agent as 'premier living' becomes a debt-ridden existence in a badly built house, the substandard bricks and mortar provide the context for the disaster that strikes this family, a disaster that is both fictional and particularly bloody. It is a fiction about the endless, inevitable, collapse of personal dreams that is also the subject of Lauren Berlant's non-fiction book *Cruel Optimism*.[40] Both detective fiction and non-fiction analysis portray the very dreams that are involved in the real-life collapse of the sub-prime housing market in the United States, its wider consequences for the global economy and the way in which the lives of thousands of people have been disrupted by these events. Michael Lewis, in his book *The Big Short*, has documented the processes through which the real-life consequences of economically unreachable domestic dreams shattered the lives of thousands of citizens of the United States.[41]

The destruction of a family in a work of fiction, based as it is on contemporary realities, helps to remind us of the strength of fantasies about ourselves, fantasies which at the beginning of the twentieth century the German sociologist Georg Simmel connected to consumption and the 'parade' of urban life. But Simmel also wrote of the way that living in close proximity 'depends on each person knowing more about the other . . . than the other directly and consciously indicates'.[42] Living in the home demands that knowledge, but a knowledge which is constantly changing as the fantasies, demands and desires of the outside world change. In the twenty-first century there can be few locations which are so invested with ever-shifting forms of *profitable* fantasy, and so receptive to them, as those of the feminine and femininity. The following chapters explore some of the ways in which these fantasies are produced, and their consequences. The argument is not that these fantasies are unique to the twenty-first century but that they have intensified. In doing so they have become a hugely significant part of the way in which inequalities, not just between women and men but also between classes and continents, are furthered and maintained.

2

Worlds of Inequality

In 1992 James Carville, Bill Clinton's campaign manager in his (successful) bid for the presidency of the United States, wrote out three slogans for campaign workers. Number two was 'The economy, stupid'. The admonition clearly directed attention to the recognition of voters' concerns about the level (and security) of wages, but it is interesting that the first slogan was 'Change versus more of the same'. The word 'change' was similarly key to David Cameron's pitch for the leadership of the Conservative Party in 2005 (Cameron promised that 'We will change the way we think'), and the need for 'change' was repeated endlessly in Barack Obama's first presidential campaign in 2008. In both cases what was articulated was a political narrative of improvement: the 'past' was generally pathologized as 'bad' and what was promised was movement towards the sunny uplands of a better world. Yet the word 'change' inevitably carries complications, the questions of what is to be changed and what is to be rejected and cast aside. That issue is as fundamental for advocates of gender equality as it is for any other politics. What should change and for whom are a central part of this chapter. The reason for returning to the question of the meaning of change is to provide some context for the forms of gendered inequality that can be named throughout the world. In general terms what will be argued here is that – despite differences of class, race, age and location – women are still generally perceived as the 'carers' for the world's citizens, but much less responsible for the public world. Equally, the condition of femininity is one that is widely exploited for various forms of profit.

Changing these – and other – aspects of the gender order continues to inspire the same degree of negative response that it did in the nineteenth and twentieth centuries. Throughout the nineteenth century, various voices condemned various versions of the 'new' woman; as vocal as male condemnation was that of women, with George Eliot amongst those who famously expressed concerns about extensive changes in the situation of women. Eliot's position has been defended as much less conservative than is often supposed, but it is difficult not to notice that whatever her views in the 'real' world, her fiction did not allow two of her best-known heroines (Maggie Tulliver in *The Mill on the Floss* and Dorothea Brooke in *Middlemarch*) to shift either the gender or social order.[1] The concluding chapter of *Middlemarch* assures readers that Dorothea, finally securely anchored in a happy domestic life, will be responsible for those 'small acts' which make life tolerable. The imaginative 'cutting down' of Dorothea, from erstwhile social reformer to the munificent wife and mother, suggests much about the fears and limitations that generations have wished to impose, often in ways that are barely known to themselves, upon the agency of women.

But alongside this fictional 'cutting down' of women who seem to transgress or challenge aspects of the gender order (and all Dorothea ever expressed an interest in doing was improving the housing conditions of a small number of tenants on her uncle's estate) is the second theme: that of the limitations on expectations, aspirations and ambitions that are individually and socially imposed on individual women, through local communities or more distant social narratives. Stepping 'out of place' and getting 'above yourself' have been consistent warnings in many cultures; authoritarian policing of communities, we might remember, is achieved both through powerful central institutions and through neighbourhoods. Not the least of these prohibitions has been that of the long-recognized pressure on women to deny, at least publicly, their intellectual ability.[2] Unwelcome as it may be to recognize, at least some of this policing is done by women, and instances can be found in cases as diverse as those of female genital mutilation or peer group regulation of dress.

Exploiting the Feminine

Throughout history it has been perfectly possible to find examples of the ways in which women have acted savagely towards other women. Those individuals, the terrifying stepmothers and wicked witches of fairy tales, are part of many cultures. More systematic, however, and a great deal more real, is the way in which the very condition of femininity has become one deeply amenable to financial exploitation. Here, for example, is Karl Marx writing about the death of a young seamstress in a London garment factory in the late nineteenth century:

> The girl worked, on an average, sixteen and a half hours during the season, often thirty hours without a break, whilst her failing labour power was revived by occasional supplies of sherry, port or coffee. It was just now the height of the season. It was necessary to conjure up in the twinkling of an eye the gorgeous dresses for the noble ladies bidden to the ball in honour of the newly imported Princess of Wales.[3]

The young woman who died is of course working for an employer who has no interest in the welfare of his employees but who wishes to satisfy the appetites of a wealthy class for beautiful dresses. The connections that Marx makes here (and the example is a rare instance of his use of an actual individual to illustrate a wider case) between social class, fashion and exploitation remain as potent today as when they were first voiced in the late nineteenth century. When we consider the conditions of work for women in the same industry – that of fashion – in the twenty-first century, we see that whilst the context is different (production and markets extend across the globe and the 'noble ladies' are more likely to be more ordinary customers) we encounter work that is as hazardous and a relationship that is no less exploitative.

Desires for pretty clothes are no less strong in the twenty-first century than in the nineteenth, nor is the aesthetic appeal of 'gorgeous dresses' any less real. The democratization of consumption now allows millions of women access to desirable clothes. But those clothes are usually produced in the global south and in appalling conditions. The people who profit most from this industry are now unlikely to live in the place of production and may easily avoid censure. The coroner who was responsible for the inquest on the dead woman who came to Marx's attention commented on conditions close to his own courtroom. Increasingly, the chain of responsibility is far more extended, as factory-based tragedies in Asia demonstrate. In these instances, what can be seen at work are the different ways in which women and femininity are both exploited.

In a first example of the appalling contemporary conditions in which 'fashion' is manufactured, what can be seen at work is the literal exploitation of women workers together with the endless, created, demands of an industry which is engaged in the unceasing redefinition of the aesthetic of femininity. The example in question is that of the entirely avoidable tragedy which occurred in Bangladesh in 2012 when the building of a garment factory, named Rana Plaza, collapsed, killing 1,129 people and injuring about 2,500.[4] The fatalities – far from rare in the world of garment factories in the global south – occasioned a worldwide protest at the conditions of work in this, and other, sweatshops.[5] (For the record, the brands using this particular factory included Benetton, Mango, Matalan, Walmart and Primark.) It was pointed out at the time of the collapse of Rana Plaza that in the same year 260 people had been killed in Pakistan and 112 in Bangladesh in similar factories.[6] But these instances of the way in which people in the global south work in life-threatening conditions in order to provide goods and services for the global north are commonplace and not confined to the garment industry. In other cases, it is less that the concept of desirable femininity constitutes an impetus to the exploitation of women workers than that the very conditions of work present a direct danger to poor, vulnerable women. For example, in December 1984 lethal gas escaped from a factory owned by the American-owned Union Carbide Corporation in the Indian town of Bhopal, killing thousands of people and maiming many others.[7] The vagueness of that account of how many people were killed arises from very different statistics: official figures suggest 3,787, while less official figures put the total at about 16,000. Neither account even attempts to quantify the numbers of people with long-term health problems that resulted from exposure to the gas. In her study of the disaster, drawing on oral history as well as written accounts from various sources, Suroopa Mukherjee traces the various global connections that led to the disaster and contributed to the fierce later battles about responsibility for the calamity. She quotes the chillingly dismissive testimony of the executive officer of the firm, Warren Anderson, one year after the accident: 'Non-compliance with safety procedures is a local issue . . . UCC can't be there, day in and day out. You have to rely on the people you have in place.'[8] This comment says a great deal about many aspects of the relationship between the global north and the global south: a determination on the part of the parent (global north) company to place all responsibility for any form of failure (however lethal) on the shoulders of local people, whilst taking absolute control of the mechanisms of profit and investment for the investors of the global north.

Mukherjee's book explores in detail the ways in which Union Carbide (later taken over by Dow Chemical Corporation) sought to evade financial responsibility for the deaths and long-term human and environmental disaster at its plant. But she also shows the way in which the impact of the disaster was gendered. Although the plant employed both men and women who died in the immediate aftermath of the disaster, the long-term impact on the reproductive health of the women who survived created a new generation of people suffering from the effects of the poisonous gas. Children were born with terrible deformities and mothers were left with entirely inadequate resources to support them. As one of the children affected by the disaster said about the likelihood of Dow paying adequate compensation: 'It would set an example for companies all over the world; they would go bankrupt.'[9] But the chances of adequate compensation were also limited by an absence of political will from other quarters. The women most affected by the disaster had few resources with which to challenge Dow, and national governments with the potential resources proved unwilling to prosecute effectively. The need for overseas investment can be a greater priority than the naming of the shortcomings of the investor, as the ban on adverse comments about civil rights in China during the state visit of its president to the UK in 2015 demonstrates. Bangladesh in 2012, just as much as the UK in 2015, was wary of any offence to sources of investment.

In the case of the disasters at Bhopal and at Rana Plaza, what we see are a number of interlinking factors. These are, first, the demand for various forms of goods for the global north, those goods being clothes in the case of Rana Plaza and batteries in the case of Bhopal, and the potential profitability of these goods. Second is the legitimation of the work in these factories on two grounds: that corporations of the global north are bringing employment to the global south and that this employment will assist in the furthering of modernizing agendas. In this toxic mix it is women who become the 'sign' of modernization, in which it becomes both possible and acceptable for women to be employed for low wages to work in dangerous conditions for the benefit of a (generally) distant wealthy elite. This, then, is one of the new forms of colonialism, and one which is often enabled by justifications about the 'empowerment' of women and the way in which paid employment is just a first step on the way to what is defined as women's emancipation.

That well-read and sagacious observer of the industrial world of nineteenth-century Britain, Karl Marx, whose observations on the connections between the exploitation of women and fashion have already been quoted, also voiced the expectation that the entry into paid labour was a precondition for the further emancipation of women. The first and greatest step towards that emancipation had been achieved, Marx had argued, through the establishment of monogamy as the only form of acceptable marriage in Judaeo-Christianity. Despite the rather more pluralist views of Marx's friend Engels (who suggested that long-term monogamy could be rather boring *for men*), Marx did recognize that patriarchal forms of marriage, in which women had no access to independent income, were less than ideal. (Perhaps Marx, often heavily dependent for material support on Engels and the small inheritance of his own wife, had some intuitive grasp of the humiliation that women could experience as a result of financial dependence on men.) But he also assumed that entry into production on the part of women would be accompanied by the greater and more solidaristic organization of labour, as well as a growing, shared understanding between men and women of their mutual dependence on employment.

This issue is crucial in thinking about gendered inequality, since the transformation that Marx predicted – that the dynamic of capitalism would sooner or later engage all adults in paid work – has largely occurred, and there are now fewer and fewer countries where a majority of adult women are not in some form of paid employment. However, various qualifications need to be made to this statement: first, we have to abandon the idea that paid work for women has only existed since the twentieth century; second, we have to recognize that both many children and many women (for example that majority of women in Europe and the United States who are mothers) are in some form of part-time or occasional work; and third and finally, there is a universal discrepancy in the earnings of women and men. Averages in this case are inevitably complex, since some work in some places is paid at the same rate regardless of the gender of the person performing it, but an overall pattern is clear: biology affects pay, and any work which can be seen to be associated with what are deemed to be biological characteristics, particularly that of women's supposed unique capacity to 'care', is poorly rewarded.[10]

The global pattern of the material rewards to women of paid work is, therefore, that women earn less than men. There is, inevitably, a minority of exceptions to this, but the general pattern is universally clear. But – and here we return to questions about women's agency and economic justice – the contemporary picture of gendered economic inequality is complicated by factors that have grown in importance since the nineteenth century. One is that the 'reach' of capitalism has been vastly extended, and extended in terms of both production and consumption. Dow Chemicals is just one of the many global corporations that control production and its rewards throughout the world. But parallel to that control of production is a second form of dominance: the way in which multinational companies seek and create new markets for their own products. Hence workers employed by companies such as Dow work within assumptions about what it is 'necessary' to pay workers, a judgement which is highly gendered. At the same time, companies seeking new markets present aspirational pictures of the 'good life'. These pictures of a desirable state of life are, as Kalpana Wilson and Lisa Rofel have pointed out, rooted in the global north and very often presented through its gendered assumptions of what constitutes 'desirable' femininity.[11] The connection here is thus: women throughout the world receive less income from paid work than men. But at least some of the paid work that many women do is to support created fantasies about the desirable appearance of women. What we see is a relationship between women, constructs of femininity and the conditions of paid work which makes a few women rich. The spider's web spun by the many possibilities of fashion and the 'good life' makes, and keeps, many women poor and in circumstances which may threaten their lives and their health.

Problems at Work

In the various ideas that inform and structure ideas about women and paid work there is a rich set of received assumptions at work. One of the most famous of these is 'pin money', that nineteenth- and twentieth-century term implying that the earnings of women were only to pay for what were defined as the frivolous wants of women. Just as this idea poured implicit scorn on the centrality of women's earnings to their own or household budgets, so many fictional representations of women (be they in film, the novel or elsewhere) suggest a long history of supposing that women's work has no value and that women 'need' very little. For example, it is only since the 1970s that financial settlements on divorce have gradually moved to the recognition of the value of the wife's work in a marriage. The achievement of this principle in both Britain and the United States has also, it should be said, occasion-ally resulted in the misrepresentation by husbands of their wealth. High-profile cases in which the wealth of husbands has mysteri-

ously 'disappeared' have provided media headlines, the majority
of which focus on the ill will of an individual husband rather than
the continuing of that structural inequality of marriage in which
work in the public world has value and that in the private world
has less.[12]

The ideological mountains that have been built out of the view
that women's natural state is that of economic dependence on
men are, however, not only those of multinational companies and
the state. The nineteenth- and twentieth-century history of the
UK and the USA provides considerable evidence that across class
lines, men − be they trade unionists or members of the professions
− voiced the opinion that women, especially married women
with children, had no place in paid work.[13] This view formed an
interesting contrast to the assumption of many better-off people
(a group which included social reformers) that their world could
not function without a considerable servant class, many of whom
were women.[14] The lives of these servants, the numbers of whom
gradually (but as we will see, not entirely) declined throughout
the twentieth and the early part of the twenty-first centuries,
depended for their security and comfort on the inclinations of their
employers.

In the twenty-first century, the idea that all adults will be in some
form of paid work has been largely universalized.[15] But two aspects
of this experience have not changed: first, the impact that the birth
of children has on women's paid employment, and second, the
resistance in many countries to the idea and the reality of providing
public resources for the care of young children. The outstanding example of this resistance is the United States: a country with
vast material resources and yet entirely devoid of anything that
might constitute federal support for either maternity or child care.
Individual employers and certain states provide certain forms of
assistance, but the absence of national, publicly funded assistance
puts the United States (as do its policies about nationally funded
medical care) into an exceptional category in the global north.[16]
But at the same time this instance also demonstrates − albeit in an
extreme form − the ideological resistance of many other parts of the
global north to providing this form of state support. The assistance
is there in the case of the Scandinavian countries and in certain ways

in other countries (France, for example, has more extensive child-care facilities than many of its European neighbours), but it is very far from generally the case that countries take it for granted that a national welfare system involves the care of young, and especially pre-school-age, children. The continuing assumption that children should be cared for primarily by their mothers remains central – and evident – to any debate about child care.

However, whilst some politicians across the industrial world are still prepared to state publicly that children are best cared for by their mothers, powerful forces undermine this view: not the least of which is that household costs (for example of housing) have largely eradicated the idea that any household can be maintained by the income of one person. But today's needs and inclinations are confronted by the same kinds of rhetoric that were part of a previous history: that women entering the workforce take work 'away' from men, that young children are harmed by care given by anyone except their mothers, that women are less 'reliable' as employees since they may leave employment in order to have children. So the arguments and assertions continue: in 2011, a British politician voiced the view that middle-class women have taken away opportunities from 'bright' working-class men, and in any year in the previous five decades of the twentieth and twenty-first centuries, a pundit can be found who has traced nega-tive behaviour in children to time spent in nurseries.[17] Women, and especially mothers, still remain a problematic category in paid work. Despite this, both Britain and the United States have initiated policies which dictate that women with children over the starting age for school are not automatically eligible for state benefits and should be in paid work, rather than in receipt of state benefits. The state, it would seem, does not recognize that care for children might extend rather further than their fifth birthday.

These examples suggest that the proponents of neoliberal policies about welfare provision are particularly hostile to thinking through questions about the extent to which any parent of young children can be in paid employment without the creation of significant forms of child care. ('Significant' in this case means day-long care which adequately covers the hours of most forms of full-time employ-ment.) The complete inadequacy of this kind of state provision, outside the Nordic countries, is one further instance – with that of the gross negligence of many global corporations about matters of safety at work – which makes glaringly clear the agendas which refuse to consider any considerations other than those of profit.

But whilst the regulation of working conditions throughout the world leaves much to be desired, those conditions are at least potentially subject to public scrutiny. That same possibility of the assessment of the conditions of work is, however, absent from a form of paid work which is dominated by women: that within the privacy of individual homes. In her book *The New Maids*, Helma Lutz writes: 'domestic work is excluded from employment law almost everywhere . . . All over the world, domestic work tends to be hidden from public view, since it takes place in a private realm in which – huge cultural differences notwithstanding – state control is taboo.'[18] Here we confront another form of the way in which gender inequality is created from factors additional to those of gender discrimination. In the first place is the general refusal of ideologues to accept the responsibility of employers for the regulation of the conditions of employment. This combines with a second factor, the universal fear and suspicion of the intrusion of the state into the private space. In this unhappy mix, women domestic workers are left vulnerable to exploitation in closed, private worlds. Lutz documents, using internationally collected material, the often appalling conditions in which domestic workers exist and the forms of separation from their own families and cultures which they have to endure. But she also, and this is a hugely important aspect of her study, makes it clear that there are gendered global connections that give rise to the employment of domestic care workers.

The first of these connections, and the most politically problematic and sensitive for some feminists in the global north, is that much of the demand for care workers results from the changing perspectives of women in the global north about paid work, together with the absence of adequate state support for these new aspirations. Put most simply, what has happened here is that a significant group of highly qualified – and often high-earning – women in the global north have found that the demands of their paid work involve an extensive need for domestic assistance, whether through housekeeping, child care or the care of other dependents. These women cannot but encounter and implicitly, if not through direct political support, be a part of a political class that is committed to neoliberalism. Even when dissenting from aspects of this ideology, they are privileged by those policies which support decreases in taxation and the diminution of both the role of the public sector and the regulation of the labour market. This form of passive collusion with the conditions of exploitation crosses place and culture; the history of the 'servant class' has never been happy and is no more so in the twenty-first century.

The reliance on privately employed domestic workers is of course the result of the absence of state-supported and regulated care provision. What is produced is a dependence on others, but a form of dependence that maintains its essentially individual nature. In many of the comments and discussions about the low numbers of women in politics in countries across the world, one of the factors that always stands out is the centrality of private wealth or childlessness of the individual woman and/or their spouse to success. This point is not just about the political direction that the views of wealthy women might take, but that of the essential employment of others to replace a woman's – but never a man's – work. In the second decade of the twenty-first century it remains the case that women in politics (or in other prominent and time-consuming public roles) are regularly asked how they are 'managing'. The implicit assumption here is that if a woman steps outside the domestic world somebody has to replace her domestic work. Margaret Thatcher always spoke of herself as 'lucky' in the support that her wealthy husband could provide for her. But she was also always astute enough to continue to maintain a mythical engagement with 'ordinary' domestic life and not to challenge any social givens about the primary location – in women – of domestic responsibilities. This picture successfully obscured the actual material supports that enabled her career, and provided a shining example of the way in which the political and social class that is most likely to employ domestic help is also often likely to be aligned to political sympathies which do not include the state-supported provision of care.

One particular example (and an example which is not unlike the many cited in Lutz's book) illustrates much of the relationship between those who employ domestic help from countries outside their own and the individuals themselves. The case is that of the British Conservative Mark Harper and Isabella Acevedo, employed by Mr Harper as a domestic help. Ms Acevedo had lived in the UK for fifteen years but was deported in August 2014. A number of points about this case are important, not least the striking callousness of the beginning of the process of Ms Acevedo's deportation during her daughter's wedding. The first point is that of the punishment of Ms Acevedo rather than Mr Harper, a burden of guilt and responsibility which is placed firmly on the shoulders of the person employed rather than on the employer. Acceptance of this principle is at odds with, for example, much current thinking in England about guilt and responsibility in the cases of sex workers and clients, in which the buyer of sexual services, rather than their provider, is potentially criminalized.[19] It would seem that in the case of Mr Harper and Ms Acevedo the protection of the employer was rather more important than that of vulnerable workers. In this instance the vulnerable worker was a woman, and although not all domestic workers are women they are generally in a majority, producing a situation in which there is no explicit discrimination against women but there is nevertheless a form of discrimination which might be termed 'associative'. That is, women are associated with certain skills – here related to domestic competence – and from the conditions of that association women become particularly vulnerable to what are general conditions. Mr Harper faced no prosecution, although he did have to resign from a junior ministerial post in government, a status which he was later to regain.

Problems of Agency

Regulatory systems which might improve the safety and the pay of the millions of women worldwide who are care workers are the kind of state intervention often termed the 'nanny state'. For anyone concerned with the question of gender inequality this form of naming is deeply problematic, not least because the term has connotations of petty-mindedness and a concern with the finer points of etiquette and behaviour that are often associated with older generations of women. It is equally problematic in that it connects with the idea that the 'nanny state' somehow encourages women to be dependants and victims. That issue – of women as 'victims' – is one that has rightly received feminist attention. In ways that are complex in their implications, the demonstration of the agency and the potential for agency on the part of women has been one of the major shifts within feminist thinking since the mid-1990s, a shift which has important consequences for how change in the situation of women is conceptualized and implemented. In a collection of papers about the subject of women and agency in the twenty-first century, editors Sumi Madhok, Anne Phillips and Kalpana Wilson wrote that:

> experiences of agency and coercion cannot be understood in a binary relationship of presence/absence, where the one is present only by virtue of the other's absence; . . . they do not map onto a dichotomy between global North and global South, as if the North is the privileged location of agency and progress, and the South a space characterised by coercion, violence, oppression and subjection.[20]

The rejection of the idea of women – and especially women in the global south – as victims is in many ways entirely correct, not least because this description has allowed women to be treated in naturalistic ways as 'weak'. But at the same time the problem with assertions about the agency of women by some authors (and not those cited here) is not the recognition of its existence but the way in which the assertion and the encouragement of this agency fit all too well with neoliberal ideas of the autonomous subject and the narrative of 'empowerment'. That narrative, which has by no means only been used in the case of women, is Janus-faced: the positive possibilities of the concept involve policies that enable individuals to acquire that personal 'capital' which enhances individual capacities and skills. The negative possibilities are those which suggest – as has been the case in the deliberate policies of neoliberal governments – that the cessation of various forms of state assistance is in some sense 'empowering'. That this is not the case has been demonstrated in the history of the UK since 2012 by (amongst others) the Women's Budget Group, which has demonstrated there is no evidence that changes in benefit regimes have done anything except extend general social deprivation and the poverty of women. In the United States, David Stuckler and Basu Sanjay have demonstrated the impact of budget cuts in various kinds of welfare provision on the health of individuals.[21] A further example – indeed, an example which applies to much of the old Soviet Union – is the impact of the post-1989 removal of diverse forms of state subsidy and state provision in eastern Europe. In her careful study of the impact of marketization on East Germany, Barbara Einhorn has demonstrated that the change from a centralized state economy to a capitalist market had many negative implications for all citizens but particularly for women, who suddenly found themselves without crucial aspects of state support, most notably that of child care.[22]

The record of the Soviet Union and its satellite states on civil rights and freedom of expression was such that it would be impossible to defend these countries as paradigms of ideal states, but what are important here are two themes: first, the neoliberal and pro-globalization assumptions that the 'free' market automatically brings with it liberal policies about gender and sexuality. Of this, at the present time, there is no evidence of a clear connection. Indeed, many countries which voice the greatest enthusiasm about the global economy and 'modernization' are the sites of entirely illiberal practice on questions of human rights. China, Russia and Saudi Arabia are outstanding examples of countries where there is considerable enthusiasm for modern technology and effective forms of industrialization but little accompanying enthusiasm for a liberal public space. The second theme – the comfortable assumption of many in the global north that 'modernization' is always a pathway to progressive forms of civil society – is demonstrably false. Consumer societies are not 'naturally' liberal societies, and there is growing evidence that the forms of power which have emerged throughout the old Soviet Union are every bit as ruthless and damaging to the population as a whole as previous forms of autocracy. Indeed, factors such as measurements of life expectancy and reports of the general health of the population suggest that, far from benefitting from the introduction of the market, many citizens of the 'new' Russia have been significantly disadvantaged, amongst whom many are women.[23]

The conventional political rhetoric about the implications of the fall of Soviet Communism was such that there was little space to suggest that perhaps state systems of welfare had had a real place in maintaining general standards of living. The new form of inequality which emerged, particularly in the Soviet Union after 1989, was no longer that of an explicitly political class, but that of a materially wealthy class which had political sympathies but less explicit public political engagement. What this class did support – and this has been the case elsewhere – is a new form of inequality which involves the making of a political language which itself has gendered implications. 'Change' is again one example of the core ideas of that rhetoric, but one which – Barack Obama notwithstanding – does not necessarily bring with it positive results for women. 'Empowerment' is another, as is the rather more ancient idea of 'freedom'. Set alongside ideas about 'freedom' are assertions about the 'stifling' impact of various forms of state regulation; regulations that libertarians challenge in the case, for example, of the right to smoke in public places or, more lethally, the quite exceptional and more randomly lethal right to carry arms that is so passionately supported in the United States. In August 2014 the *Guardian* newspaper published details of a children's book, written and published in the United States, that supported the right of all citizens to carry arms and of the good sense of encouraging children to follow this path – a not unfamiliar call to citizens of the United States, but publicized with the slogan 'How to raise a son that feminists will hate'.[24] This slogan suggests not just that gender wars still flourish (a reading which can be immediately confirmed by any day's version of the UK newspaper the *Daily Mail*'s so-called 'Sidebar of Shame', a rigorous online policing of the appearance of largely female celebrities) but that they are constantly re-enforced.

Locations of Inequality

There are various strains and stresses, including that of gender wars, that might be connected to the reality of living in neoliberal market economies that are increasingly socially unequal, and these have been noted since the publication in 2009 of Kate Pickett and Richard Wilkinson's *The Spirit Level: Why More Equal Societies Almost Always do Better*.[25] The book suggested a causal connection between the degree of social inequality in a society and its degree of social cohesion. Social inequality, the authors argued, does not produce positive social results. The book was published before 'austerity' policies (enacted across Europe after the financial crash of 2008) took hold; then the inequality which Pickett and Wilkinson had observed became, in some European societies, much more evident. These 'austerity' agendas provoked both political and academic responses: for example, the Occupy movement, and its dramatic slogan about the '1%' who owned the greater share of the world's wealth, achieved global recognition. At the same time a number of academics, amongst them the group already mentioned which includes Danny Dorling, Thomas Piketty and Ha-Joon Chang, voiced the collective, although individually nuanced, view that capitalism is no longer 'working'. One of the factors that all these authors pointed to was the global increase in social inequality and the social tensions provoked by aspects of the state withdrawal from welfare provision.

All these books are a testament to the recognition that, in both moral and pragmatic terms, gross social inequality is – for both individuals and groups – a disaster. Every respect is due to these authors for stepping away from neoliberal economics and suggesting that there are other ways to build and run societies. What is perhaps more problematic, however, is that the mindset within which these eminent and praiseworthy academics operate is one in which the key social institution to which individuals belong is the household. (This is stated, for example, on the second page of Chapter 1 of Dorling's *Inequality and the 1%*.) There is a certain justification for thinking about household income, not least because the household is the place where many people live. But to think of a population *only* in this way obscures differences between women and men and – to return to a fiercely fought battle about welfare payments in the UK in the 1970s – implicitly enforces what was once known as the 'cohabitation' rule. This rule was attacked and successfully defeated by feminist pressure because it explicitly assumed the financial dependence of women on men, and limited the extent to which women could be paid independent welfare benefits.[26]

Similar battles about payments in the UK of Child Benefit had been waged since the introduction of the benefit in 1946. Any government, prior to the UK coalition government of 2010, which had attempted to make Child Benefit a part of household income had been defeated. But in 2010 the household returned to the operation of the UK benefit system: benefit payments are now calculated on household income, and Child Benefit is no longer paid exclusively to mothers. At a time when other forms of state provision are under attack (services providing forms of care most particularly) and when it is the individual who is at the centre of political ideologies about the 'workshy', it is the household, long known as potentially unequal in gendered terms, that has become the state's chosen location for material support. What this produces is the masking or the disappearance of those gendered household inequalities that have been documented since the nineteenth century. Amongst those most important inequalities is that of gendered differences in income: the way in which the importance attached to household income removes attention from the low pay of part-time workers (generally women) or the low pay of workers in the care services (again generally women) who are prepared to work 'unfriendly' hours because of child–care responsibilities. An apparently prosperous household, in short, is not necessarily a materially equitable household. Moreover, it is simply unacceptable to find writers with admirable arguments about social inequality who refuse those aspects of gendered social inequality which potentially affect half the population.

Support for the idea of the household as the foundational unit of society nevertheless sits well with many people, since it endorses those crucial familial relationships that are an essential part of their world. To challenge that idea appears to fly in the face of the experiences of those millions of people across the globe for whom family is the central part of their lives. Yet it is not so much a question of whether or not, and how, people live in and value families as one of the idealization of the patriarchal, nuclear family that is invoked by those on the political right. Not for the first time, in contemporary politics the term 'family' is most energetically used by those who wish to distract attention from both the world outside the front door of the household – the world in which individuals enter paid work and have to take their place in various forms of competitive environments – and the world within, which remains, for all too many women and children, a place of abuse and danger.[27] Invoking the comfortable (and comforting) idea that the household is always a place of harmony and equitably shared resources is entirely consistent with the interests of neoliberalism, since the aggregation of household income (and other resources) minimizes and disguises the differences that exist between individual family members. Here is one of the great paradoxes of neoliberal politicians: the public endorsement of the view that those famous hard-working families are threatened by rogue individuals, and yet the refusal to recognize that families are made up of individuals, all of whom contribute to the family in different ways, not least because their capacity to do so is structured by factors both inside and outside the household.

Most significant amongst those factors is the persistence – as we have seen – of the global association between women and care. Yet in the face of all the evidence that demonstrates and supports this connection there has emerged, since the mid-1990s, a literature that suggests that gender relations within and outside the family have now changed considerably. In that context Anthony Giddens argued, in *The Transformation of Intimacy*, that new forms of gender relationships had emerged in intimate relations: women's greater engagement in paid work had decreased financial dependence on men and provided a basis for genuinely consensual relationships.[28] Without embarking on a lengthy discussion of this account of social transformation (questions, for example, about the evidence for women's greater financial independence and more equal gendered responsibilities for care are glaringly absent from the book), what is important about it is its articulation of what many people would like to be the case: namely that radical change or indeed revolution in the relations between women and men can take place without bothersome legislation and regulation, state structural support for those who care, or any modifications in the expectations of men. Yet at the same time as this comforting thought is suggested, so too (perhaps even by the same individuals) are panic-stricken

fears voiced about the ways in which young women are achieving precisely those forms of success which promise independence
from male provision. Hence minor fluctuations in the relative
rates of success for girls and boys in the academic *rites de passage* of
the English school system are read as evidence of a new world of
female dominance. Looking at the ground rather than the heights
is one of the many ways in which public attention is kept firmly
away from a larger view of the social system.

What is made out of a reading of one country's school examination results illustrates that second form of change in gender
relations that is widely canvassed. This is the twenty-first-century
version of the bundle of ideas about the evolution of a new form
of womanhood that has beset any form of change in the behaviour
of women for centuries, perhaps most famously in the case of that
'new woman' who so worried eminent writers such as H.G. Wells
and Arnold Bennett in the early years of the twentieth century.
What is consistently made of changes – however minor – in the
ways in which women comport themselves is that these alterations constitute a threat to social stability. Moral panic about the
possibility of instability in the gender order is not something that
is unique to the twenty-first century; indeed, many European
societies have remarkable histories of concern about women
getting 'out of place'. From the women who criticized Simone de
Beauvoir in Germany in 1936 for wearing lipstick to the women,
whether famous or not, who receive vicious internet threats
today for what is seen as their transgressive engagement with the
world, conservative ire is consistently voiced against women who
seem to be asking for different forms of social arrangement about
gender.[29] But what this does not mean is that conservatives and
neoliberals are always, and uniformly, against certain forms of
women's agency. It is possible to hear, across time and place, the
roars of enthusiasm that greet women who are endorsing national-
ist or conservative or neoliberal views; those women, the 'good
women', who are successful in business or who succeed in ways
that do not seem to challenge the gender order.

So as much as it might simplify the political categories in which
we think ('good' liberals or 'bad' neoliberals), it is also important,
certainly as far as thinking about gender relations is concerned,

to recognize that conservatives and neoliberals are not cohesively and automatically opposed to the agency of women or to rethinking certain aspects of gender relations. That there is a greater coincidence of support, for example for gay marriage, amongst those who are on the left of the political spectrum rather than those who are on the right may be the case,but not, importantly, always the case. Nor is it the case that women themselves always endorse policies that support aspects of change in gender relations. For example, on abortion (in both Europe and the United States) there are many women who are passionately opposed to policies of 'choice'. The campaign for the right of female ordained Anglican priests to become bishops had many women opponents, as did – in the early years of the twentieth century – the British campaign for women's suffrage.[30] These examples suggest that it is entirely incorrect to assume that women have political and social views in common.

In the complexity of political views about gender and gender relations across the political spectrum, there is thus no certainty about either many aspects of the situation of women or their political unity. Women are divided, as has often been pointed out, by class and race, but what is suggested here is that women are equally divided in terms of their relationship to ideas about the individual and the collective. To think of oneself, and to act within that conception, as an autonomous person is as possible for some women as it is impossible for others. To make yet another leap, to thinking of oneself as a woman, allied to other women rather than to one's own family, is a leap of equal – and perhaps equally terrifying – proportions. But at the present time, a time of enduring material inequality and hardship for millions of people across the globe, establishing political and collective links of association outside either the autonomy of self or immersion in the interests of the family remains inherently difficult, not least because the family remains, as it has always been, a place of both support and constraint. In the attack on state spending and state support for gendered forms of the care for others, what we see is that people are driven back to the family: if there is no support for the care of elderly relatives or any financially viable child care, then it is the family to which individuals turn. Hence, of course, the now-recognized time that grandparents (if largely grandmothers) are devoting to the care of their grandchildren.[31] This was always a recognizable feature of child care throughout the world; the change is that it is now a feature of the lives of relatively well-off sections of the population for whom costs of essential services make paying for child care increasingly difficult.

Thus do neoliberal policies and governments valorize the continued existence of the family, not just in their political rhetoric but in the knowledge of the support that families can provide for the lived consequences of these policies. To say that neoliberalism is breathing new life into the importance of the family is perhaps too much of an exaggeration, since the family has, in different ways, been supported across class lines for centuries.[32] But certainly, the resistance of neoliberalism to accepting that care for others is a social as well as a personal responsibility is enhancing the continuation of the functional importance of the family, beyond the conventional expectations of its role in the care and socialization of children. However, the term 'the family' in this rhetoric is little except obfuscation of the fact that it is largely (although certainly not always) women in the family who are replacing non-existent state or entirely unaffordable private services. This result of neoliberal policies has received considerable attention, and stating it here is to remind, rather than to suggest discovery. Yet one less commonly noted consequence of this widely recorded aspect of neoliberalism is the way in which the pressures and scale of family 'needs' (be they for the old, the young, the sick or the physically impaired) change not just how women spend their time and energy in the private sphere, but also how this increase in domestic responsibilities alters the way women can act in the public sphere. Those windows of opportunities through which women might actually be able to live the life of metropolitan 'singledom', take part in politics or other aspects of community life, are, for many, increasingly limited. The birth of children, the frailty of parents or any of the circumstances that can impinge on individual autonomy can change this life dramatically.

Novelists – and clearly the imagination of some politicians – can dispose of the needy at the stroke of a pen, but their carers in the real world cannot. Hence it is central to the concerns of every country in the world to recognize how calls for the further 'empowerment' of women, and their participation in paid work, are more than slightly at odds with what is emerging, as a result of neoliberal policies, in the decline of state-provided forms of care, as a form of the *extended* domestication of women. That is to say, it is not just that all adults (regardless of their responsibilities for care) are expected to be in paid work, but that responsibilities outside the realm of the labour market increase. It has often been noted, of the global north, that women were brought into paid work at the time of the two world wars and then equally enthusiastically returned, by coercion or more subtle shifts in the labour market, to the private sphere when the crisis had passed.[33] In the second decade of the twenty-first century, the crisis in question is not one in which the nations of the global north are under general physical attack. But it is a form of crisis, in that the political narrative of neoliberalism has so widely denied the legitimacy of state support for care that women's participation in the labour market is at best being constrained and at the worst made impossible. The considerable implications of this consequence of neoliberalism have yet to be fully recognized by its adherents. In addition, what has not made its way to the inner reaches of the neoliberal mind is the recognition that women without income, or with little income that is 'disposable', can consume. Consumption, as every economic pundit has known for decades, is central to the viability of capitalism. Removing, or limiting, the spending of women can have a powerfully destabilizing effect on the collective economic health of a country. It is not for nothing that the financial pages of every newspaper across the global north voice constant concern for that place called the 'high street'. The rise in internet shopping has weakened the literal relevance of this place, and turned real-life high streets in many towns and cities into graveyards for the products of the redundant fantasies of fashion. Nevertheless, shopping, wherever it takes place, is a crucial barometer of a country's economic health. To paraphrase: if we do not shop, it is not us but the economy which drops.

We might, as women confined to the home by care responsibilities, shop online. Indeed, it might be a crucial way in which we maintain the fantasy that we are part of the world outside our front door, but the question of how we pay for those goods still raises its ugly head. That 'candy-floss world' (to use Richard Hoggart's ever-evocative term),[34] of which shopping is a part, is a place that cannot be entered without income; it is the derivation of that income that has always been problematic for the majority of all populations and for women in particular. But at the present time, the gap between the manufactured fantasies of who we might be and our ability to engage with those fantasies is becoming even more considerable. Not only do women everywhere earn less than men in often – literally – precarious situations, but the very consumer fantasies epitomized in the lives of the wealthy, which remain as absurd as they have ever been, are now generalized through the aspirations of celebrity culture. Exaggeration and hyper-unreality are positioned against gendered forms of increasing poverty and constraint.

3

Problems of Subjectivity

From the 1960s onwards various western states embarked upon, first, a rewriting of the legal arrangements of marriage, second, a redefinition of the legal code about forms of sexuality, and third, a more general – although often with legal implications – rethinking of the socially tolerable written and visual forms of the representation of sexuality. All these reforms, frequently the subjects of campaigns stretching back to the nineteenth century, were achieved through the efforts of both women and men.[1] Even if the efforts of men (in, for example, the resistance to the infamous British Contagious Diseases Act of 1864) were a result of the better opportunities for men to be part of legislatures, there is little doubt that there were often very effective coalitions of women and men engaged in these important campaigns for changes in the law and practice. It appeared to many that the so-called 'permissive' societies of the west established new, and more liberal, boundaries about individual behaviour.

Imagining the Female Body

But that sympathetic endorsement of the impact of the liberalization of laws about sexual behaviour attracted critics, not all of whom were associated with the political right. These critics were inclined to see these changes less as steps towards greater human freedom and more as forms of potential individual and social loss. Writers such as the sociologists Zygmunt Bauman and Herbert Marcuse, steeped in those European traditions that fused Marx and Freud, were critics of what Bauman was to call 'liquid love.'[2] Bauman's work (*Liquid Love* was first published in 2003) is later than that of Marcuse (whose *Eros and Civilisation* was published in 1964), but the arguments are very close: that 'free' sexuality and the 'freeing' of sexuality from social conventions and restraints do not necessarily bring freedom, but enable a form of anarchy which is all too easy for commercial interests to exploit. Neither man is arguing for restrictions on sexual choice, abortion or divorce, but what they are both concerned with are the questions about the implications of different forms and contexts of social control, and in particular those connections with social order that George Orwell had identified in his novel *1984*. Again, neither Bauman nor Marcuse wrote specifically about gender relations (although Bauman refers briefly to the work of Judith Butler), but the importance of their work lies in that willingness to ask questions about the possibility of a crucial relationship between changes in our ideas about our individual subjectivity and other aspects of social existence.

One very important aspect of this question, central to the work of Michel Foucault, is that of the surveillance of the individual, and in particular the way in which surveillance is as much a matter of our internal policing of ourselves as the literal one of the architecture and technology of surveillance.[3] Watching others is not simply a matter of those, literally, concrete forms which allow a panoptic view of the members of a given institution. Apart from the extensive growth of implicit and often unknown surveillance through new forms of technology, and those ordinary forms of daily life such as mobile phones, the extent to which individuals now survey themselves has become a remarkable aspect of the twenty-first century.

The site of this energetic self-policing is, for the majority of citizens, the body, a place of all kinds of deep personal concern and anxiety. The prospect – and indeed the encouragement – of self-surveillance on a massive scale meets any woman who encounters any form of the media: what need for the literal force of the panopticon when a new, more fluid and eminently exploitable form of surveillance can be produced through the values and aspirations both implicit and explicit in, for example, the headlines of a magazine.

The woman, who might be any of us, who looks at magazines or watches film or television or surfs the web is often, evidence suggests, thrown into a variety of responses by the myriad of images that confront her. One of the first might be that of purchase, of consumption of the magic potion which will abolish the impact of age or ageing, or the underwear which will equally immediately remove the appearance of excess weight.[4] The second, and a very much more damaging, response, is that of the kind of dangerous self hatred that has been the object of much feminist (and other) discussion.[5] In the case of the first response, the worst that can happen is that it will become rapidly clear that the magic of cosmetics is unreliable: neither the signs of age or those of overeating will disappear with the certainty that has been suggested. Money is down the drain, but at least the individual is left with feelings of participation in an apparently worthwhile search for beauty and the sense, especially dear to Protestants, of having done their best. But with the second response the psychic element is more complex, since the question still remains for individual women of how they are going to compensate themselves for feelings of failure and inadequacy. We know that young girls (and increasing numbers of young boys) may self-harm and become anorexic, but we also have to consider a wider, more shared form of self-harm: that of the belief in the healing and transformative powers of the pursuit of a perfected body.[6]

To explore this question of the way in which current representations of the female body and women's sexuality can encourage, if not actually initiate, forms of self-harm in women, it is not necessary to move further than to the websites of the *Daily Mail* (for readers in the UK) or *People* magazine (in the United States). In both those contexts, what we find is a conceptual world that seems to suggest that the lives of contemporary women are dominated by two things: their body weight (or, in cases such as that of Kim Kardashian, its contours) and the extent to which they may be 'loved up' with a significant other; that significant other being generally a man. On any day, the 'news' on these sites provides graphic illustrations of women who have 'lost their baby weight', grown a larger 'bump', sported a 'toned' body or appeared in public looking 'effortlessly chic'. Individual women have also demonstrated the physical costs of overeating or apparently defied the process of ageing. All aspects of the appearance of the female body are meticulously catalogued; no situation, however mundane, fails to be policed; and even if we omit those many photographs which are clearly acts of collusion between photographer and the person concerned, it still leaves a considerable proportion which seem to suggest that the female body somehow possesses qualities that are inherently, consistently and unequivocally sensational. Sadly, this is less in the sense of the recognition of the aesthetic possibilities of the female body than in the many ways that it can fail, often dramatically, to live up to dominant, highly specific norms. But those very cameras which bring us those images reliably add weight and girth, a point clearly recognized by those whose livelihoods are dependent upon appearing in front of the cruel lens. Thus what is taken to millions of women as an ideal is the repetitive image of those skeletal women who in no way accord with the female population as a whole. But for that population what is also presented is a fantasy of how it might look. Increasingly, that fantasy bears little relationship to actual body size in much of the west: according to estimates of the average weight of people in industrialized countries considerable numbers of people (between a half and a third according to some statistics about some places) are clinically obese. The language which accompanies these statistics is often that of the battleground; we are 'fighting' epidemics of obesity, 'challenging' our 'unhealthy' lifestyles and 'condemned' to early deaths. Whole islands may sink under the weight of their population. Little of the everyday furniture of our lives – from aeroplane seats to coffins – is apparently large enough for the human beings that use them.

We can explain the body weight of many people in the west by reference to diet (too much fat and sugar) and a sedentary lifestyle. Those are perfectly sane and sensible explanations: human beings will reliably gain weight when their days are physically inactive, with a diet replete with sugar-laden drinks and food. But whilst this allows us to understand the considerable size of the obese, it has little to say about the collective anxiety about body size and body image that can contribute to those patterns of eating that in themselves create the conditions of obesity and anorexia. Every day, in the press and on television, there is evidence of the way in which the female body is defined, implicitly, as a problem and a place in which the owner of a body is at war with herself. Insofar as we inhabit this problematic place, we are beset by regimes that begin with an initial fierce assessment and self-abasement, to be followed by various punitive programmes for reform and redemption. Our bodies are too fat and too hairy in the wrong places. So the hair on our heads has too little 'body', our faces have lines on them and we suffer from an absence of 'toning' and 'firmness'. In fact, the phrase in the Anglican prayer that declares 'there is no health in us' seems to sum up particularly well both our own and the contemporary media's view of the female body, in which the critique of the body is conducted in a language ridden with moralistic assumptions.

Any glance at any urban centre in any part of the world will demonstrate that very few women seem to have taken to their hearts the authority of mantras of self-improvement that are now part of everyday existence. Indeed, quite the contrary: what is remarkable about looking at people in most parts of the urbanized west is not their preoccupation with how they look but rather their total *lack* of concern about this issue. Apart from specific metropolitan locations where the very rich and/or the affluent young congregate, the predominant urban style suggests little attention has been paid to any advice about how to dress or how to improve an individual body. But this very fact makes even more alarming the evidence which we have about the amount of money that is spent every year, across the world, on cosmetics and other forms of bodily 'improvement' such as trips to spas or beauty 'treatments'.[7] It would seem that individual women – who collectively spend a great deal of money on the hopes of cosmetic improvement – are locked into an endlessly unfulfilled relationship in which their love and their hopes for themselves come to nothing. The expensive jars of face cream sit on bathroom shelves across the world, just as the DVDs of exercise routines gather dust, both a daily reminder of the victory of hope over experience. This is a form of narcissism which takes us beyond the classic ending of the sad story of Narcissus, in which the silly young man falls into the pond. In this case, women everywhere are encouraged to stand gazing at their imperfect reflections, chained to expectations in which everything is asked of them and nothing is given.

But of course a great deal is given to those who manufacture cosmetics, run spas and produce fashion, all of which represent just a part of the various means on which women pin their hopes for self-improvement.[8] In addition there are the much more expensive and much more potentially dangerous forms of medical intervention, the pills and the cosmetic surgery on which aspirations to endless youth are pinned. Self-love in these contexts comes at a high price, not the least of which is the admission that an individual body has somehow 'failed' to live up to the ideals of the moment – ideals which, as historians of fashion point out, can change from decade to decade. Yet what is important here – quite apart from the massive confidence trick that the cosmetic industry perpetrates every day across the globe – is the way in which an entirely appropriate form of love, the love for ourselves that allows and builds both self-respect and respect for others, is perverted into a form of failed and constantly failing imperfection. We can never stay young; like the most up-to-date clothes we are all, sadly, doomed to our own built-in obsolescence. When Marx spoke of our 'alienation from our species being' he was not referring to the fashion and beauty industry. But the idea is entirely apt for the ways in which we are persuaded away from the real needs of our bodies, for work that does not degrade or kill and an environment which does not poison, to fantasies which we can almost never fulfil.

Other Bodies

The unavoidable limitations and frailties of the human condition have been observed by every society that ever existed, and have done much to help to build religions that emphasize continuation, rebirth and resurrection. However, one of the consequences of what is mistakenly called 'secularization', and might be better described as the decline in public religious observance, is that we have come not to worship the deities of religion, the perfect beings that we are not, but to make ourselves into our own gods, in which process we have come to torture ourselves for our own imperfections. As we internalize values about what the perfect woman is and what the perfect female body looks like, we accept for ourselves the burden of suffering for the body and its desires, quite as much as any of those Christian martyrs and saints who believed that the ruthless discipline of the body was a way to the truth of religious experience. In a curious way – and hence here the scepticism about 'secularization' – we have taken this idea about the spiritual gains of suffering and used it to structure the way in which we approach and understand our own appearance. The vocabulary about beauty and women suggests some of these connections: beautiful women are referred to as 'goddesses', and jocular references to beauty treatments are made in terms of suffering and endurance.

In the theology and the vocabulary of all the Abrahamic religions there is an individual God. We might make ourselves into our own prospective gods: those people that we could be if only we ate less or used better face cream. But there is also another spectre here, not just of the person we might be but also of the person who will help us to confirm who we are. Traditionally, and still conventionally in many parts of the world, that person for women has been a man, and 'winning' a man's love has been constructed as a positive achievement for women. Gaining heterosexual love has its own language of loss, triumph and success: whether seen from outside or inside the heterosexual world, a person listening to descriptions of love might suppose that the 'getting' of love is a military campaign, a place of conflict and aggression. Women – again in some

contexts rather than others – no longer have to marry in order
to have children or to be financially supported, even though it is
a form of magical thinking to suppose that being an adult single
person now fits easily into social norms. The case in the UK of
the prosecution in 2010 of Christopher Jefferies for the murder of
Joanna Yeates demonstrated that prejudice against single elderly –
and somewhat idiosyncratic – people remains alive and well. Thus
a single man who lives by himself is the classic dangerous 'loner'
not just of detective fiction but of actual police prosecutions; in
that same fictional genre 'lone' women find it necessary to explain
their situation.[9]

The need to attract a man, despite the various shifts in public
discourses about sexuality in the west, still constitutes a form of
considerable social pressure for women. Young women, evidence
suggests, are particularly vulnerable to this pressure. Although it is
now over thirty years since Adrienne Rich published her famous
essay on 'Compulsory Heterosexuality', it is apparent that normative pressures towards heterosexuality remain powerful.[10] The
pressure is not simply to achieve a relationship with an individual
man, but to adopt that form of the self where the appearance and
behaviour are such that they attract male approbation. Whilst
allowing that expectations about appearance and behaviour have
considerable variations across lines of race, age and class, there is
nevertheless a unifying dynamic at work here: that an important
part of all that work on and financial investment in the female body
is about a positive male gaze. This relationship between project
(the female person) and judge (male regard) suggests that the prop-
osition of Gillian Rose in her last, remarkable book, *Love's Work*,
that in modernity 'we have become infinitely sentimental about
ourselves, but methodically ruthless towards others', somewhat
underestimates the degree to which we have become ruthless not
just towards others but also towards ourselves.[11]

That ruthlessness most usually takes the form of our judgements about ourselves and – for women – our judgement about
our appearance. Women's judgements about each other are
probably no more, or less, generous than they have been in the
past, but what contributes to that greater ruthlessness of which
Rose speaks is what is described as the 'sexualization' of western

culture. The debate about sexualization is often in terms of the impact on very young children of clothes and forms of entertainment that have conventionally been the preserve of older people. The young girl who appears at the infant school party wearing a T-shirt which proclaims 'So many boys, so little time' is the stereotypical picture of what sexualization in a culture can achieve. In this, the always problematic innocence of children is perverted into a distorted form of aggressive adult heterosexuality.[12] But these outward manifestations of sexualization, crass, vulgar and ridiculous as they might be, are straightforward compared to the actual dynamic of what is described as 'sexualization', a debased contemporary form of what has always existed in all cultures: a recognition that human beings are – as their very existence demonstrates – sexual beings, in which the lines between innocence and experience have always been energetically socially policed. Yet what aspects of the contemporary western world have made of the implicit sexuality of infants and young children – a reality which Freud made a part of our everyday understanding – is the determined erosion of the boundaries which were central to his work between the imagined and the real world. In this, it is all too easy for capitalism's endless search for profit to see new opportunities for markets through deepening and extending the time frame of heterosexual 'success' and 'failure' to include the lives of children. This very real aspect of sexualization is often overlooked in modernity's enthusiasm for sensation and scandal. Within this it is easy to write stories for the media about four-year-old girls in high heels or boys of eleven who have become fathers. It is less easy – and much less in tune with what are assumed to be the tastes of the public – to question what commodified forms of sexuality, particularly heterosexuality, are actually for. Once we start to challenge this, we challenge empires built around heterosexual angst and engagement.

That last sentence should not be read as a statement which assumes that gay relationships are devoid of the same rich emotional possibilities as any other form of sexually charged relationship. The so-called 'gay pound' demonstrates all too clearly the thinking which assumes that all forms of personal, intimate relationships can be packaged for commercial gain. In this, and to return to previous comments about sexualization, what is occurring is the extension of the values of the market to all aspects of personal life and behaviour: the bodies of women, children and men, which were once a rich source of plunder for necessary manual work, have now become the place where work of another kind takes place. This new 'body work' is not just the work on our bodies which we all do but the manipulation of the ideal of the body, so that its needs are never stable but always a changing panorama which demands new solutions and new products. For example, it would have been (largely) unthinkable fifty years ago for women to suppose that it was in some sense 'necessary' to police their bodies for the condition known as cellulite. Indeed, women's magazines of the 1950s made little mention of this now apparently rampant scourge. Today, sections of pharmacists' shops are devoted to yet another bodily 'battle' against this hazardous threat, and it is an endless point of discussion in terms of the bodies of female celebrities. Without the entire transplant of legs or arms (or other forms of surgery so massive that they would involve as yet unknown expertise), there exists no sure cure for this aspect of ageing.

This is not to suggest that entire female populations have become so besotted with concern about various parts of their bodies that this dominates our lives. As suggested, a glance around any country in the world demonstrates that this is not the case, and that the 'battle' which women are supposed to be fighting on a daily basis for control over their wayward bodies has for some either never been started or been well and truly abandoned. What is important, therefore, is that – largely because they do not have the resources of time or money – the majority of women do not engage in extreme forms of body care or engagement. But a culture has been created, and has been created with increasing energy since the end of the Second World War, in which the appearance of the body is an expected and legitimate site of anxiety and concern. It is this heightened concern about the body which has come to have such an impact on women, and to provide such large profits for the companies which make cosmetics, fashions, various forms of diet aids and the whole panoply of products through which the body can apparently be 'improved'. We have not, therefore, become more sentimental about ourselves. On the contrary, we have become ruthless towards ourselves quite as much as towards others, a ruthlessness which expresses itself in the potential narrowing of love for both ourselves and others. The imperfect person who faces us every morning in the mirror is the person whom we are persuaded to dislike for its failure to live up to always changing cultural expectations of perfection. As 'reinventing' ourselves becomes a social pressure, an endless search for the correct position within an ever-shifting zeitgeist, we are encouraged away from a lasting relationship not just with ourselves but with others.

Some of these themes have been explored by Bauman in his *Liquid Love*, a book in which, as suggested, he explores some of the consequences of what he describes as a world without stable bonds of intimacy. The book contains little specific discussion of the appearance of the body, but a passage about consumerism is apt here: 'Consumerism is not about *accumulating* goods (who gathers goods must put up as well with heavy suitcases and cluttered houses) but about *using* them and *disposing* of them after use to make room for other goods and their uses.'[13] If we apply this passage to the discussion of women and both their own bodies and those of others, what it helps to illuminate is addiction to that hamster's wheel of fashion and fashionable appearance which can play such a negative part in our lives. Consumerism, as Bauman argues, is not just about acquisition; this is not a relationship with goods in which we acquire them simply for their future potential value. On the contrary, what we must do with the fashionable clothes that we have bought is to display them and act, endlessly, as if we believed in the rhetoric of the fashion press, in which every autumn is the 'new' season and a time at which we too might become miraculously transformed. To be 'so last year' is the most critical comment that the fashion press can use; as the German sociologist Georg Simmel wrote at the beginning of the twentieth century, 'Every growth of a fashion drives it to its doom, because it thereby cancels out its distinctiveness.'[14] It is a comment which accords with the work of Lauren Berlant about disappointment and 'cruel optimism'; the endless hopes that we entertain for that better world which we are unlikely to obtain.[15] Not only do the goals of everyday life constantly change, but they change in ways that are beyond our control yet constitutive of our shared existence.

How the Body Matters

What Bauman also describes, as well as the dynamic of consumerism which creates those new cemeteries of hope now made real by charity shops, is the implication for personal relationships of the energy and vitality of consumerism. If we throw away our clothes, it is difficult not to consider that social relationships might also be discarded. Here, Bauman reminds us of the British soap opera *EastEnders*, in which the longest relationship lasts about three months. We might argue that a soap opera could not exist if all its characters stayed for years in stable relationships (although this is very much so in the long-running British radio soap opera *The Archers*), but, allowing for that, it is noticeable that this fictional form of rapidly changing relationships is mirrored on both sides of the Atlantic in 'celebrity' magazines. Vows of everlasting love turn to dust with endless frequency; every cross look between partners is recorded. It is hard to decide from reading these pages if the apparent impermanence of human relationships is merely inevitable or to be mourned. Ever since a famous picture of Princess Diana in which she very openly displayed her boredom with her husband, any celebrity wishing to maintain a positive view of her or his relationship has to adopt a mask of complacent pleasure and delight when in the company of the significant other. Since the endings of relationships (in both fiction and reality) are now achieved as much by women as by men, it would seem that at least one form of gender equality has been achieved. It is no longer only men who seek escape from what Simone de Beauvoir once described as the apparently 'natural' 'boredom' for men of heterosexual monogamy.[16]

Real women, who exist outside soap operas, might well maintain that none of this fiction matters, that the bonds of the 'real' world are such that the imagined version is merely escapism or a form of the confirmation of the better sense and judgement of the 'real' world. But the impact of the media invasion of the imaginative space which we all possess about ourselves and our world is accepted in terms of other values implicit in forms of fiction: those of violence, racism and misogyny. Thus it seems perhaps overoptimistic to suppose that we can retain, in the context of intimate relationships, such clear boundaries between fiction and non-fiction; Bauman seems correct to argue for the increasingly fragile nature of human relations. Rather than dismissing or accepting this thesis, however, what we might also do is to suggest that it does not go far enough: that the pressures against stable relationships are being deeply and significantly intensified by aspects of some of the deliberate policies of market economies. These policies (which include mantras about 'growth' and 'new' jobs) are not explicitly about human relationships, but since they constantly invoke fantasies about re-creation, remaking and the availability and the value of the 'new', it is difficult to suppose that they do not impact in some ways upon relationships other than those of consumption. Perhaps the increasingly fragile and problematic love, for others and ourselves, of which Rose, Bauman and others speak is not just as great as he suggests, but actually greater and in important ways gendered. Not the least of those ways is that of contemporary uncertainties about gender identities.

This returns us to that twenty-first-century woman in front of the mirror, perhaps gazing despondently at the reflection. The world in which this woman lives is one of ruthless self-examination in terms of various forms of social expectation. Some of those areas (how to look, what to wear) might contain elements of choice, while others – how to be in paid work, how to maintain relationships – are increasingly prescribed, as government policies throughout the world write tighter and tighter rules in terms of access to state benefits and other forms of state support. What we know, as certainty and fact, is that the policies of neoliberalism are making it almost impossible to do some of the things that various aspects of love and long-term commitment might involve. For example, many people might wish to care full time for a dependent partner or child or friend, but doing this is largely unsupported by any meaningful state benefit. At the same time, on another page of the balance sheet of everyday budgeting, the basic costs of existence (housing, costs of basic utilities and transport) consistently increase. 'When poverty comes in at the door, love goes out of the window' was a saying known to many British communities in the first part of the twentieth century. Our assumption in the latter part of that century, and the first part of the twenty-first, however, is that we now live in the material circumstances which can support what we describe as love and recognize the various ties and responsibilities that come with it. It is not the case that this enabling situation has completely vanished, or that the majority of either the British population or that of the United States has been thrown into absolute poverty. But what has increased for all except the most fortunate is what Judith Butler, writing of the context of war and forms of national life, has called 'precarious life'.[17] Equally, a social class called the 'precariat' has been identified, across the globe, as that increasingly large number of people who live with daily concerns about how to maintain everyday existence.[18] Even for those people outside this endlessly insecure existence, we cannot but recognize that we are daily asked to encounter those 'interesting' times which the ancient Chinese were alleged to have regarded as a curse rather than a blessing.

In this situation there can be no doubt that both men and women are affected by conditions of economic insecurity. But here the question is how this situation impacts upon women, and how gender plays its part in creating not just actual forms of gendered poverty but gendered strategies and forms of negotiation for facing material concerns. The mythical ideal woman of most forms of the media (be it in advertising, film or any form of visual representation) is a person who is young, urban and autonomous. Endless individual stories about those young women, generally heterosexual but with some acknowledgement of gay women, are the basis of that part of the media which is not devoted to various narratives about male-against-male conflict and violence. In these narratives about young women, two themes predominate: the uncertainty of a heterosexual relationship (will he/won't he love me?) and women coming to the recognition that a heterosexual relationship is an essential part of adult life, which should be recognized as more important than any other concerns. For decades it has been a consistent theme of Hollywood that if women attempt to move outside the conventions of the heterosexual world, particularly through the ambition of asserting their own values, they will have to learn the error of their ways. Women getting above themselves is a theme that has enthralled Hollywood for generations. Ever since Katherine Hepburn had to be shown the error of her (moralistic) ways in *The Philadelphia Story* and *The African Queen*, there has been a general insistence that the problematic factor which defines women who 'get above themselves 'is their assumption that they can live without men or are to be allowed to judge them. Hepburn in *The Philadelphia Story* is taught a lesson, but a lesson constructed through deceit. The point of the ending of both that film and *The African Queen* is that it is appropriate for women to surrender judgement to men, however morally flawed those men might be.

Questions of Order

If we follow the reading so far of the output of Hollywood (together with that of much of the rest of the world), it allows us to see that what is at stake in much of the media, and the much longer traditions of other forms of representation, is the question of the order, and the ordering, of gendered power and the possible limits of its transformation. In the twenty-first century it is widely recognized that Shakespeare's *The Taming of the Shrew* is a problematic text, and much effort is put into readings that emphasize the conclusion as a triumph of consensus rather than coercion. But this re-reading (which can be exercised on all forms of canonical works) has its own limits: that of how far judgement and in particular moral judgement can be released from the stranglehold of gendered power. This issue, of how to transcend what is perhaps the most important implication of biological difference, is central to the making of intimate relationships. For centuries, patriarchy assigned authority in heterosexual relationships to men. The twentieth and twenty-first centuries have challenged this social organization of love and desire as unacceptable, not least because violence towards women in intimate relationships has become a matter of public concern and responsibility. In recent years too, ideas about the potential coercive dependence of intimate relationships have provoked calls, such as that by Foucault, for the separation of sexual desire from personal ties and obligations.[19] Being 'free' to love did not involve for Foucault, as it had done for some early twentieth-century women who campaigned for women's access to contraception, freedom from unwanted pregnancy. What was being suggested here was another form of that existential freedom about love and desire which certain of his compatriots – notably Jean Paul Sartre and Simone de Beauvoir – had also done much to explore. But the issue opened up gendered disagreements between Beauvoir and Foucault.

Those politics of sexuality and desire with which Foucault was associated (in which sexual desire could exist for itself and by itself and not in the context of other forms of human emotion and association) were vehemently opposed by Beauvoir.[20] Relations between the two were 'cool', and although Beauvoir herself had done much to argue for women's freedom to love, independent of patriarchal norms and laws, she rejected what she clearly interpreted as an unacceptable form of freedom. Beauvoir always maintained that sexual relations could not exist separately from the person; for her – with her central focus on heterosexual relationships – the issue was not one of separating sexual desire from social relations but of ensuring that the social relations of sexuality were not organized in male terms. But this clash between two notable individuals is more than a vignette of the intellectual life of France; it also relates to questions about gender, love, desire, spontaneity and the relationship of all to the possible transformation of the political, and gendered, order. More recently, Jacqueline Rose has explored this question in her essay on Rosa Luxemburg, writing that: 'It is often argued on the left that the darkness and fragility of psychic life are the greatest threat to politics. Instead, through Luxemburg, we might rather see this life as the shadow of politics, or even its handmaiden, an unconscious supporter in the wings.'[21] It could of course also be argued that the 'darkness and fragility' of psychic life terrify not just the political left but the political right as well, and that an inordinate amount of attention, today and in the past, has been devoted by repressive, authoritarian regimes to controlling the various possibilities of the sexual desires of their citizens.[22] But like every other instance of social life, the social control of psychic life and the expression of sexuality is gendered; it is impossible to think of any clearer manifestation of the projection of male fears about women's sexuality than that of female genital mutilation. This literal attack on women's physical health (albeit often achieved with the active collusion of women) is condemned by individuals across the political spectrum and is part of that more general darkness and fragility of which Rose writes. The less physically violent forms of constraint on the dress and social association of women in other parts of the world similarly suggest the terrors of the supposed incontinence of male heterosexual desire. In both cases, it should be loudly said, it is women who are the human forms through which male desire is policed and who are made responsible for male sexual continence.

In this context, what is so important about Rose's account is the wish to bring together, through a discussion of Luxemburg, those themes of the feminist postcards and slogans: the personal and the political. Luxemburg's theory of the place for spontaneity in politics is famous,[23] and no doubt still strikes fear into the hearts of those politicians who above all else demand the subjection of the individual will and conscience to the constraints of party discipline. Throughout much of the literature on Luxemburg, and other far more conventional women in politics, what can be detected is a tradition which sees women who become involved in any form of public life as inevitably encountering personal loss and unhappiness; biographies of Emma Goldman have, until recently, consistently emphasized her fractured personal relationships. When the American political scientist Martha Nussbaum wrote in 2013 of the need to bring more 'love' back to politics, we might interpret this in part as a call to allow politics to be informed by the more positive aspects of the emotional world; equally, Nussbaum's work can be placed within that literature on 'affect' which argues for a much greater recognition of emotions in public life.[24] But at present, for women arguably more than for men, reconciling love, desire and the public, political realm remains politically problematic. Most importantly, and on both the political right and the political left, this suggests that women in politics are considered to be a threat to social and political order. Women and femininity represent, to much of the public world, irrationality, chaos and the whims of nature. That relationship between women and nature and men and culture, first proposed by Sherry Ortner in 1972, still retains its potency, not least in the various ways in which women and men are constantly forced to order, for public consumption, their private emotions.[25]

From this, we might suppose that those who control various forms of access to the public sphere (largely men) have consistently imagined the presence of women in public institutions as disruptive. This fantastical disruption could take not only the form of concern about the subjects that women might bring to the political agenda (for example, questions about caring responsibilities), but also that of the much more problematic question of what it actually is that women represent in the public, male imagination. Arguably, that female person remains, for both gay and straight men, a figure who is symbolic of two generally unresolved questions in the human psyche: how to love and how to admit to the vulnerability that love presents to us. We might attempt to separate, as was Foucault's thesis, love and sexual desire, but even with this separation there remains what the sociologists Ulrich Beck and Elisabeth Beck-Gernsheim have described as the 'normal' chaos of love.[26] Some decades before Beck and Beck-Gernsheim, Max Weber had written that 'This boundless giving of oneself is as radical as possible in its opposition to all functionality, rationality and generality.'[27] Love, as all these authors are pointing out, is by its very nature a bringer of chaos to the ordered person: the literature of love suggests a disordered willingness to die for the other, think of no other and surrender all to love. This is not a condition generally associated with either public order or the needs of the state. We might, therefore, think of Foucault as both a prophet of disordered desire and a perfect spokesperson for the place of love in a neoliberal society. As such, he might represent that form of permissive sexuality which is actually less disruptive than ordered love. Unregulated sexuality (albeit taking place within the confines of 'safe' sex) is much less socially disruptive than the claims of individualized love, carrying with it the messy baggage of families, divorce and ties to others.

But, increasingly, few in the public political life of many western societies would support rigid norms about adult sexuality. What remains for most is a 'normal' chaos about love, and a chaos that is formative of those issues about women in public that continue to beset the planet. As is the case in other contexts, the global north generally congratulates itself on its acceptance of women politicians and speaks with enthusiasm of those other parts of the world which have female leaders. But examine the public discussion of these women more closely and what emerges is an intensely controlling rhetoric about their individual characteristics. Numerous writers have pointed out that women in public life are invariably discussed in terms of their age and appearance, their domestic situation and, more often than not, the problems that they have faced in entering politics. Modernity, as Elizabeth Wilson has pointed out, might assume a commitment to the emancipation of women (and to a certain extent fulfil that expectation) but still retains various forms of constraints on the behaviour – and the appearance – of women.[28] What can appear as a sympathetic engagement with the 'problems' of women in public life seldom includes the suggestion that these problems might be generally recognized and abolished; men are seldom asked how they achieve success, be it political or otherwise. The imagined paths of men and women into public life would appear to take two distinct forms: the former a straightforward career, a line leading ever upwards, and the second, for women, a curved and tortuous path, always at risk from the slings and arrows of fortune. Feminism has often read those slings and arrows in terms of the absence of help with care or of straightforward discrimination, and whilst both of these causes are anything but negligible, the psychic energy with which women's public place in the world is resisted suggests that something more is at work than the refusal of certain social arrangements of care.

The terrible, and horribly effective, energy of the resistance to the presence of women in power has manifested itself in various ways over centuries, and continues to find new forms as means of communication and locations of power change. For example, the 'new nastiness' to women in the west which has been recorded has taken the form of threats, sometimes murderous, on the internet. As a consequence of the abuse she had received, in 2014 the academic Mary Beard asked the entirely apt question of why it is that any woman who, in her words, 'puts her head about the parapet' is likely to be shot down and/or abused.[29] That abuse can sometimes be construed as trivial (criticism of what individual women wear), but it is also sometimes literally brutal. It suggests, indeed, both a narrative of hatred for women and at the same time an underlying fear of loss, of the disappearance of that imagined, loving, acquiescent woman who is at the centre of so many human fantasies, be they held by women or by men. In short, since the general human condition is that of being born of women, it is impossible for any of us not to have fantasies of – as Melanie Klein pointed out – both love and hate about our mothers; fantasies that are generally resolved into various forms of acceptance.[30] If we fear that this idealization of the calm and always forgiving mother is about to be taken away from us through public women who question men, or who seem to love generally rather than specifically, or who hold power, then we may translate our fears into various forms of aggression against those women.

These suggestions are emphatically not to explain away any of the gross abuses (whether through vicious posts on the internet or the explicit refusal of the basic human rights of respect for the person or participation in civil and political life) to which women are subjected. These aspects of human behaviour are simply wrong, wherever they occur. But what is important here is to locate the causes of that behaviour, and to establish the connections that link that behaviour with socially produced internal worlds. These connections have always been central to post-European-Enlightenment aspirations, and certain groups of intellectuals, notably the Frankfurt School, have contributed considerably, but often problematically, to that tradition. Building on the work of their compatriots Georg Simmel and Max Weber, they examined – as Freud had done – the complexity of the ways in which individuals form their attachments, be they personal or social. All these writers importantly emphasize the question of authority in social life, but whilst often critical of various forms of bourgeois authority they make little or no attempt to deconstruct the reasons why so much more authority, across the globe, should be automatically invested in men rather than women, or invested only with difficulty in women. That debate and discussion have belonged to latter generations of psychoanalysts (notably Jacques Lacan), whilst anthropologists – for example Henrietta Moore – have given us cross-cultural accounts of the ways in which differences of biology endlessly accompany differences in public and private power.[31] In the global north we might mock this, as in the *Punch* cartoon set in a committee meeting at which a man comments: 'That's an excellent suggestion, Miss Triggs. Perhaps one of the men here would like to make it.' But if we only regard this as a joke we forget those many occasions on which the voices of the powerless are ignored.

There remain two ways in which we have to confront our gendered perceptions and narratives about love for ourselves and for others. One is to recognize that in order to understand the part that love and self-love play in the reproduction of gendered inequality, we have to abandon our sentimentality about the relationships that love that can create. We assume that when we form families, or households, or friendships, we do so on the basis of equality and enter those relationships freely. We also assume that being able to form those relationships is implicitly (if not explicitly) free from expectations and assumptions about patriarchal authority. That this might not be the case – that we bring to those relationships extremely powerful cultural and personal baggage that is disposed not just towards male authority but also towards the conventional resolution, through heterosexuality, of the Oedipal triangle – opens up the question of the way in which constructions of our psychic world seldom escape from what Gilles Deleuze and Felix Guattari have called 'familialism'. In an essay whose title invokes Marx and Engels's essay of 1844, *The Holy Family*, these authors discuss what they see as the domination of culture by the expectations that the implications of the Oedipal relations between parents and child will be resolved in ways confirmed by Freud, and subsequently integrated into many aspects of socially sanctioned normality and morality.[32] Deleuze and Guattari write approvingly of the work of Gisela Pankow in which schizophrenic patients are helped thus: 'It is a question of giving the patient tactile and other bodily sensations that lead him to a recognition of the limits of his body . . . It is a question of the *recognition* of an unconscious desire, and not of this desire's satisfaction.'[33] This discussion – and other aspects of the work of Deleuze and Guattari – is concerned not explicitly with gender inequality but rather with the ways in which gender difference is maintained. What is relevant here – and what can be developed from their work – is threefold: one issue is their own suggestion that canonical aspects of psychoanalysis are crucially a theory of the gender order, which have been integrated into mainstream western culture in ways that continue to reproduce the dominant psychic status of the father. This thesis can be demonstrated many times over in social ideologies and practices, as well as institutional forms, which either explicitly or implicitly endorse the primacy of male interests. The second issue here is that of the social implications of the reproduction of patriarchy: it is not simply that literal fathers are often given a psychic primacy, but that forms of desire and the various structures which either support or articulate desire are formed through the centrality of the father. To give this idea reality, we might relate it to the previous discussion about the energy which is directed towards engaging and maintaining heterosexual desire, an activity in which women play an active part. Women globally are encouraged (with various degrees of coercion) to dress and behave in ways that attract men. The third issue here returns us to the subject of Marx and Engels's *The Holy Family*, in which the authors condemned what they described as 'half measures' in contemporary Germany.[34] Their denunciation of what was to become, later in the nineteenth century, a tradition of forms of state intervention suggested that the choice of ameliorative measures, rather than the recognition and abolition of fundamental causes, would simply prolong what were construed, in various ways, as 'problems'. Yet as state intervention in the lives of its citizens became a dominant political rhetoric of the twentieth and the twenty-first centuries, aspects of the tradition of feminism were to play a part which the following chapter will suggest has become problematic, in terms of the way that certain feminist interventions can prolong rather than decrease social and gendered inequality. Here, I shall suggest, are two other reasons why this intervention is questionable, both of which are connected to the theme of love.

The first link we can make between the question of state intervention and the issues of love and feminism is through the way in which, as generations of most known societies and psychoanalysts have persuaded us (or attempted to persuade us), both women and men must ideally come to love through heterosexual desire. That this is no longer enshrined in the legislative order of most of the west or much psychoanalytical practice is entirely to the credit of those who have campaigned long and hard for this dissolution, and who are still forced to campaign against brutal and absurd forms of heterosexual orthodoxy elsewhere. But, and it is a very large but, as much as a greater liberality of the boundaries of sexual desire has been allowed, there still remains a constant reiteration in much of western political rhetoric of an expressed concern with the norms of the heterosexual 'family', the importance of biological fathers, and what is seen as the 'problem' of the greater integration of women into both positions of professional success and social power. This politics, which often includes accounts of largely statistically insignificant changes in aspects of the western world, continues to suggest that the transformations that have taken place in the experiences of women (be they of autonomous control of fertility or forms of access to paid work) are somehow problematic in terms of social order. Of these narratives, two issues are salient here: the first is the sense of mourning for lost worlds which is sometimes present, and the second is the importance of recognizing and assessing the degree of collusion between these narratives and the interests of all men. In certain cases, and certainly in some cases of significant forms of power, men's resistance to any change in the gendered order is visible and unequivocal. But in other contexts masculinity does not function – as Raewyn Connell has pointed out – as an undifferentiated and homogeneous whole.[35] Nor, as Rahila Gupta and others have argued, is it possible to continue to see sexuality only in terms of the binaries of male and female, masculine and feminine. The politics of transgendering and the transgendered subject is a challenge to all assumptions of 'secure' gender identity.[36]

Confronting our expectations about the proper place of women and men is not, therefore, a question which is solely either for men or for women. It is a question that confronts all of us because of the way in which we construct our individual perceptions of desire, both metaphorical and literal. Those radical women (of either the political left or the political right) who have famously engaged in politics have, as we have seen, often been the subject of abuse. Many have had to resort to defensive strategies to ensure that their political aspirations are not defined as in some sense threatening.

But in this consideration what we also have to note is the way that in aspirations about social improvement, about the kinds of 'half measures' that Marx and Engels identified, there can be found powerful expectations about what women can, and cannot, do. An illustration it is perhaps useful to cite here is that of the case of a man's reactions to the participation of a woman in rethinking the arrangements of the social world. The man was Leonard Woolf (the husband of Virginia Woolf), and the woman was Beatrice Webb, the early twentieth century social reformer and a major force in the foundation of the reforming political group of the Fabians. Leaving a lunch party with Beatrice Webb and her husband Sidney Webb, Leonard Woolf wrote:

> One of the worst Webb meals to which we have been . . . Mrs Webb began to talk almost at once about the Reconstruction Committee which she is on. She talked incessantly and every tenth word was 'committee'. She has apparently succeeded in inventing a committee for babies, a committee for lunatics, a committee for the sick, a committee for the disabled and a committee for the dead; but the scheme for the Cosmos is not complete because she has so far failed to invent a committee for the able-bodied and unemployed. However, she still has hopes.[37]

Perhaps understandably, the Woolfs found that they had little to contribute to the conversation.

But Leonard Woolf's comment about Beatrice Webb (and other remarks about her follow a similar, if sometimes more admiring pattern) contains within it much that is fascinating and important about the ways in which social reform in the twentieth century had to operate within ideas about the proper extent and form of state intervention. At one end of a continuum about the legitimate reach of state intervention there is Beatrice Webb, doyen of state planning, whilst at the other are libertarian critics of the 'nanny state'. In both cases, what is at stake is not just sets of ideas about the degree to which a state should assist (or meddle, according to a different view), but human feelings both about others and about our proper relationship to social order. At the beginning of the twentieth century, and at about the same time as the Woolfs were having lunch with the Webbs, Max Weber was writing about the question of bureaucracy and the degree to which it can become an 'iron cage' in which we have to live. Weber was far from being a critic of bureaucracy per se; he was well aware of the democratic merits of bureaucracy in complex societies. But he also had, as did – in the same historical period – Rosa Luxemburg and Emma Goldman, an understanding of the ways in which the attraction of social order and cohesion can produce extreme and unwelcome forms of order.[38]

In this debate about the merits of order, which as even the most radical libertarian will agree has at least some place in all societies, the part that is played by the existence of gender differentiation as a form of social order has often been minimized. Sometimes too, and for what are seen as progressive reasons, differences between women and men have been denied. Although questions of and about the place of sexuality in social order have been recognized by a long tradition of writers from Wilhelm Reich to Judith Butler, more central is that of the day-to-day representation of the ways in which we associate male and female with certain sorts of emotional states, for example those of desire, comfort, agency and rational competence. 'Everyday' sexism, as it is nowadays described and documented, demonstrates that we still live with very rigid expectations of the identification of all these capacities – about care, love and desire – with either men or women. A look at the history of women in the political life of the twentieth century suggests some of the ways in which the relationship between women, passion and politics both has remained consistent and is at the same time being constantly rewritten. It also allows us to speculate about the similar way in which the issues of the centrality of the image of the father and the familial are constantly being renegotiated but always reaffirmed. For example, the rhetoric of much of politics in the first decades of the twenty-first century is about 'protection' and 'security'. Both these states have long-term associations with the expectations of responsible male adulthood. Women – and men – are expected to care for their children, but it has been a consistently male responsibility to care for other, female, adults. This kind of subliminal expectation may no longer dictate behaviour (if it ever had so great an importance as is sometimes supposed), but it nevertheless informs debate and public views about the gender of the military and forms of national security and political engagement.

This discussion began with a return to, and a reaffirmation of, the thesis that it is very difficult for societies to transcend an identification of human biology with certain expected human characteristics. Despite the ways in which the meaning of gender is constantly being renegotiated, and patriarchal control in certain parts of the world significantly diminished, gender differences are in many ways no less developed and assumed as 'natural' than they were at any point in the past. But this has occurred as much through market forces as through social liberalization. The visible richness of western consumerism encourages us to believe in the endless possibilities of the ongoing project of our own human transformation. Because we have seen, within living memory, our lives transformed in terms of longevity and resistance to disease, we have accepted that we are – to use the unfortunately highly gendered title of Daniel Stedman Jones's book – 'masters of the universe'. But this belief has implicit problems for the gender order. The long association of women with nature (and men with culture) is being increasingly challenged and interrupted by various forms of technology and women's increasingly universal engagement in paid work. With this comes the question of who might be the focus of male control and power. The fury of aspects of contemporary misogyny might be considered in terms of the ways in which what men saw as the legitimate authority of culture, and once exerted over those very individuals, is now eroded by changes in women's relations to the natural.

These shifts in the symbolic relations of men and women to nature and culture might help us to understand the considerable evidence about male physical and verbal violence to women. This material demonstrates that male anger about and to women persists and is likely to occur both in peacetime and in the context of war and armed conflict. But we do know that it is publicly less acceptable, a recognition that has rewritten some of the rules about conduct in public. Political life is one aspect of public life, and hence it is helpful to use the example of the history of women in British politics, and through this to speculate about how intersections of gender, desire and agency have expressed themselves. At the beginning of the twentieth century, Beatrice Webb was a prophet of rational social improvement and against what she identified as 'screeching' women, by which she meant suffragettes. Her political persona was that of the thinking woman, the woman who could make (and win) her case by what would be seen by those in political power as rational argument. But in doing this (and as a striking contrast to the evocation of passion in politics which could be seen in her contemporaries Emma Goldman, Rosa Luxemburg and Alexandra Kollontai), she became a model for other women in politics that remains to this day. It was, and is, a model which, in its construction of desirable female political personhood, is organized around a massive overestimation of the degree of rationality in male politicians. Throughout the twentieth century, and to this day, there are numerous examples of the ways in which male politicians have explicitly used emotional rhetoric to make their case, in the face of which those who have regarded it as what they might have termed 'emotion' have been rendered powerless. The most tragic aspect of this refusal of the recognition of the passions of politics was in reactions to German fascism, an ideology and an accompanying public display of passionate unity which paralysed the thinking of many in Europe. At the time of writing, a similar case might be made out of support for the policies of the United Kingdom Independence Party (UKIP), the very name of which is, in many rational senses, ridiculous. But that party draws its energy from an emotional space in which people fear, hate and distrust those unlike themselves and seek identity and community only with those similar to themselves. The same reactions to the threat of unknown and different 'others' are apparent in the support across Europe and in the United States for the exclusion of those outside narrow definitions of the acceptable citizen.

The cases of UKIP and of other forms of vocal xenophobic and racist politics may seem to be something of a diversion in a discussion of gender, desire and politics. There are, however, close links between these questions. One of the policies through which UKIP attracts supporters is its manifest hostility to changes in the gender order, be it institutional adaptation or the acceptance of multiple forms of sexuality. It is clearly frightening for many people, both male and female, that this aspect of individual, intimate lives should be publicly legitimated and enlarged. Yet paradoxes abound here. One of the most common oppositional arguments about same-sex marriage and/or civil partnerships is that both challenge conventional expectations about marriage. At the same time, however, these changes extend a form of social relationship – that of marriage – which has long been an indication of conventional respectability. It is absurd for a party which invokes such fear of change to resist a form of change which offers an extension of the conventional order. But the rich seam of allegiance to the idea of the natural social order of biology supports, on both sides of the Atlantic and throughout the world, a lasting commitment to the view that male and female biology can only be lived out in certain ways. When these ways are changed or challenged, it is clear that deep emotional fears and concerns are unleashed. But today what we face is not merely that conservatism about gender that has always existed, but an enhanced sense of vulnerability to possible changes in the ways that women and men exist with one another. As the conquest of the natural world has been assumed to be greater than ever before, the departure of women from 'natural' forms of womanhood has become the focus of greater concern. Indeed, a historical overview of this shift could consider that when forms of control over nature (vulnerability to famine and disease, for example) were minimal, there was much less energy exercised about the public policing and control of the sexual behaviour of both men and women. Whether or not this suggestion stands up to empirical examination is a matter for debate; what is beyond debate is the very considerable and often vicious energy that is now directed, in various ways, towards women's assertion of agency and that capacity for 'choice' which lies at the heart of so much neoliberal rhetoric.

The preservation of various forms of the gender order has become, in the late twentieth and early twenty-first century, a matter of increasing political importance; indeed, the question of whom we should desire and with whom we should have sexual relationships has, arguably, been higher up the political agenda than ever before. For many, feminist and gay rights movements are directly to blame for this, and for that reason they are the subjects of attack throughout the world. The passion with which the heterosexual order is maintained and fought for might surprise visitors from another planet or even from that fictional androgynous future which novelists have created. In Britain and in the United States, there has been furious opposition not just to legal changes which allow gay people to marry but also to that legislation (and its preservation) which allows access to abortion and contraception. Outside the global north, similar kinds of opposition persist; indeed, in some countries the mere idea of gay marriage cannot be publicly voiced. In instances of the treatment of victims of rape, it has similarly become clear that underlying fears about women's sexuality and the right of men to define and control it still persist.

From this evidence, existing in various forms throughout the world, we can conclude that the control of female sexuality remains a subject of passionate concern and is not, in any sense or in any location, a historical phenomenon which the globalizing forces of the 'modern' world have erased. Countless individuals and powerful institutions remain energetic about how other people 'do' sex. But here we might also recall the power of our imagination – that place where people have constructed their own future and that of others – and the way in which the power of what we fear can become so overwhelming. All the evidence, over hundreds of years and many places, is that human beings are often terrified of the possibilities of sexuality, not least of their own. Once we allow that this is the case, we can locate one of the reasons for those continuing exercises in regulation which are imposed on women in terms of their dress, public and civic participation and rights. This cumulative evidence would suggest that those feminists who have argued that global misogyny is the single explanation for gender inequality have an overwhelming case. That this is not so – and that gender equality will never be achieved through this view – is the subject of the following chapter.

4

Enter Feminism

Feminism entered this narrative on the very first page. A more extensive engagement with the complexities of feminism at this rather later stage in the discussion is needed because the dynamic underlying the creation and the re-creation of gender inequality was thought to be central to our understanding of feminism, its meaning and the hopes that we might entertain of it as a resource on the path to gender equality. Baldly, the case here is the argument that feminism – whilst it has helped to create the space in which we can discuss ideas about gendered social inequality – has nevertheless had a far from straightforward relationship with the making of gender equality, and that in some important ways it may assist the various forms of social inequality that support and sustain gender inequality.

Conditions for Feminism

Feminism has only been able to exist – and this remains the case – where the public discussion of gendered inequality is possible. Speaking and demanding are essential parts of any political movement, but both words hold all kinds of complications. 'Speaking' involves a public space in which to speak, a space in which those who speak can ask for change and are not immediately either punished for or prohibited from making those demands. This 'free' public space, however, which should be a part of all societies, is far from universal and women have been, and are, subjected to all kinds of constraint for asking for changes in gender relations. That last sentence also introduces the power relations of many societies: women have to 'ask' for changes in gender relations; there is very little evidence to suggest that in this context straight men have *ever* had to make specific demands for changes in gender relations. But men have, of course, been vocal in their demands for social change and have been joined in radical and revolutionary campaigns by women.

So the first essential factor which has to exist for women to be heard is the acceptance of the idea that all citizens have a right to voice their opinions, whether through speech or through the various forms of the written and representational worlds that now exist, although far from universal in their availability. Nor does the fact of the availability of the technology of various forms of communication mean that the use of it is not subject to censorship and various forms of surveillance. It is all too easy for governments to ban public meetings and to exercise various forms of surveillance over the behaviour and the expression of opinions of their citizens. But there is no necessary relationship between the degree of surveillance in a society and the control of dissenting opinions: the UK is estimated to have a greater degree of public surveillance than anywhere else in the world, but at the same time there still exists considerable public space in which citizens can voice their opinions.[1] On the other hand, a society which has very little technology of surveillance may make it very difficult for women to voice their opinions and their demands, simply because there is no public space (public meetings, the media, institutional politics) to which women have access.

Thus for feminism – in whatever shape or form – to exist there has to be a form of civic society in which citizens can freely express their views about the people and the ideas which govern them. That form of society is also dependent on other factors: an urban space, with at least a significant number of people who are literate. The 'mob' which was once thought to be at the heart of revolutionary movements in the eighteenth century has now been shown to have included many urban, often literate people who had effective ways of communicating with one another.[2] The surveillance of dissenting others became a key concern of the state in the UK as long ago as the sixteenth century; the perceived threat of Roman Catholics to the English state laid the institutional foundations of the idea that the interests of the modern nation state would be served by locating possible forms of destabilization. It was a practice that was echoed throughout parts of Europe and in other countries with a strong sense of the needs of the central state for absolute control of its citizens.

By the nineteenth century, many states – both in Europe and elsewhere – had developed various institutional forms for the investigation and punishment of dissent. Protests by women, whether through the written word or through public meetings, were sometimes – in the case of the treatment of some British suffragettes – met with extreme forms of cruelty, but also with indifference and ridicule. Those women in the early twentieth century (Kollontai, Goldman, Luxemburg) who were subject to the greatest severity were seen as dangerous because they were revolutionary socialists rather than campaigners for women's rights. It was only when the suffragettes in England began to be visibly disruptive and attack various forms of property (especially in London) that the brutal aspects of the energies of the state were introduced and brought to bear against individual women, often with considerable and vicious determination. But there were no bans on written material, women continued to write and protest, and there was no proscription of travel by suffragettes or, for example, of the collecting of funds to support the cause of suffrage.[3]

That historical case, of the campaign by women in England for the vote, is the first instance in the UK of the use of the possibilities of the dramatic in feminist politics. English suffragettes recognized that the early twentieth-century media had an appetite for the sensational; consequently, to be 'sensational subjects' would bring attention to the cause. Even so, throughout the nineteenth and into the twentieth century, feminism was a cause fought largely through the written word. That words can themselves be dramatic is always and entirely possible, but the degree to which feminism throughout the twentieth century was actually disruptive of social order was almost nil. Women wrote novels and non-fiction, submitted evidence to all manner of committees, organized petitions and established women's organizations. But until the last decades of the twentieth century there was little evidence, anywhere in the world, of feminism exploring the potential within the everyday world for sensational events of any kind. When these events did emerge they were, in retrospect and compared to other forms of political action, minimal in their physical threat.

For all that, various forms of disruption by women – be it angry and subversive intervention at a Miss World Contest or a number of women driving cars in Saudi Arabia – is often treated with what can only be described as hysterical over-reaction.[4] That a bag of flour thrown at a Miss World judge can become a matter of serious public concern, as if the very axis on which the planet revolves has suddenly been threatened, says much about fears concerning the fragility of the gender order. The response to minor acts of resistance on the part of women has often been disproportionately severe, from which we can suggest that there is a global pattern to resistance and protest by women: that the refusal of women's rights to take part in the public sphere is supported by the belief that any such participation would immediately destabilize the social order. Yet apart from the acts of civil disruption by suffragettes, the bags of flour thrown at the judges of beauty contests and marches in the streets of liberal democracies, the history of western feminism has largely been a written history, in which no Bastille has been stormed or tea thrown into a harbour. The most famous recent public protest by women – and one that was ferociously punished – was that by the women of Pussy Riot, singing subversive songs in a Russian church in 2012. For this the classic Russian punishment of exile to a work camp was then invoked. The absurd spectacle (although anything but absurd for the women concerned) of a massively powerful and highly militarized state feeling so threatened by songs in a church that it had to bring its whole punitive weight to bear on those concerned says something about the terror that subversion in women can provoke. But it is the sheer sense of vulnerability that accompanies the punitive viciousness of this mindset that is of interest, not least because of the tradition within feminism that always attempted to provide reassurance for it.

What will be described here as the 'tendency to reassurance' in feminism has a long history, one in which women critics of existing forms of gender relations feel obliged to offer their agendas for change in terms which suggest the benefits to men of these changes. The tradition begins with Wollstonecraft, whose plea for the better education of women argues for it in terms of the benefits that this will bring to men; a tradition energetically embraced and articulated by John Stuart Mill and throughout the nineteenth century. Fiction by women in Britain in that period echoed some of that reassurance; at the same time as women writers such as George Eliot spoke for the recognition of the moral integrity and autonomy of women, they also did much to reassure their readers that this would improve rather than reorganize gender relations. It is not until we reach the figures of Sylvia Pankhurst and the socialist trio of Kollontai, Goldman and Luxemburg that we come across women who are prepared to argue for changes in gender relations, and in the structural factors that produce both social and gender inequality. None of these women doubted that these changes would not be of benefit to men, but they were prepared to argue for the autonomous rights of women, a tradition which is often marginalized by the way in which state benefits for women are reinforced by their positive impact on others. Thus campaigns in the UK about child health, maternal well-being and child benefits have traditionally been couched in terms of the particularity of the relationship between mother and child and the benefits to the state of healthy children. It was this latter relationship which was so vividly discussed by Anna Davin in her groundbreaking essay on the poor health of British working-class men at the end of the nineteenth century. Whilst this connection – between mothers and children – conforms both to traditional expectations and to empirical reality, it also continues and re-enforces the conventional expectations that state assistance to women should above all else enable their altruistic relation to others. For example, writing in 1939 in her study of working-class women in Britain, Margery Spring Rice invoked the argument that improvements in the living standards of these women would give 'freedom and honour to those who perform the most indispensable labour of the world'.[5]

Throughout the first part of the twentieth century, a major theme in feminism – as in cultural politics more generally - was that of women's relationship to modernity, within which women both demanded 'emancipation' and were enthusiastically criticized by others for rejecting conventional expectations. Those who did not accept the legitimacy of this possibility of greater emancipation were numerous in the early years of the twentieth century. British authors attacked and pilloried what they defined as the 'new woman', and some, such as D.H. Lawrence, expressed grave reservations about the shift that could take place in the heterosexual sexual relations between 'new' women and men. In both the United States and Britain, the figure of the wife who torments her husband with never-ending demands for money with which to consume became a new form of what misogyny had long constructed as the 'nagging' wife; in 1922, Sinclair Lewis proposed, in his novel *Babbitt*, the first and very powerful account of the gendered tensions of living in a world of mass consumption.[6] But modernity, in various contexts such as the cinema, art and architecture, had at its core an aesthetic which no longer presumed the stability of exaggerated and explicit forms of femininity and masculinity. Women's clothes changed to allow the wearing of trousers, short hair and the shirts and ties, parodic of masculinity, that became associated with writers such as Radclyffe Hall, Alice B. Toklas and Vita Sackville-West. This aesthetic was not, however, universally accepted in all its forms, and many aspects of the aesthetic of gender continued to be expressed in traditional ways. This cultural tension is, and was, important for the subsequent development of feminism because it initiated a pattern in which the ways in which women dressed became part of engagements with the 'modern' and modernized public space, whilst at the same time that same public space accommodated many powerful refusals of other novel forms of gender. Those countries in the global north outside explicitly fascist regimes were more likely to allow unmarried women to enter male spheres of employment (the classic opposite case being that of the refusal of Hitler's Germany to allow and encourage women into paid work in the war economy),

but for all that, the promise of modernity as an emancipatory ideology of gender was one which for women throughout the world
was only ever partially fulfilled.

A Secondary Sex

As we have seen, one of the few people who detected this refusal
was Virginia Woolf, herself one of the most important voices of
literary modernism. In her novel *Orlando*, Woolf had made the
suggestion that the way we 'do' gender might be a product of
circumstance and culture rather than nature; an idea which was
to be developed in what was to be one of the most powerful texts
of feminism of the twentieth century, Simone de Beauvoir's *The
Second Sex*, first published in 1949. Writing in her diaries about
the genesis of this work (a project originally suggested to her by
her colleague, lover and friend Jean-Paul Sartre), Beauvoir had
said that she had never herself experienced any prejudice against
her and that all the men with whom she was friendly had always
treated her with complete equality.[7] As an example of statements
suggesting as much the denial of the impact of gender differences
as the denial of the privileges of class, this one must be close to the
top of any list; reading Beauvoir's own autobiography is to read of
a woman intellectually formed and professionally assisted by men
who was unable to see the advantages given to her by her success
in male hierarchies. The question which she clearly never asked
was why, in that final examination in which Sartre came first and
she was ranked second, the examiners had decided on this position.
Later feminist scholars have, however, done much to challenge
that ranking and to document the strength and the originality of
Beauvoir's work.[8]

The *Second Sex* stands, and has done so since its first publication,
as a centrally important text within feminism. But in terms of its
heritage for feminism, there are perhaps two aspects of its thesis
which are problematic: the binary divisions between women and
men, which exist throughout the text, and the almost complete
absence of a recognition of the structural forms of the social world.

The book was written by Beauvoir in the years just after the Second World War, and many of the social circumstances which were taken by Beauvoir as indicative of the ways in which girls are socialized were those of her own upper middle-class childhood in the France of the first decades of the twentieth century. In those years, France, like other European countries, was attempting to come to terms with modernity, but it was a comprehension and accommodation which were very far from complete and had done little to change, by 1949, the central characteristics of much of France outside the metropolitan area of Paris. These characteristics included the relatively underdeveloped technology and industrialization of the country, its limited urbanization and the absence of women from even that most limited form of political participation, the right to vote. Indeed, writing about women in France gaining the vote in 1945, Beauvoir voiced the view that this was of little interest to her since she knew that her politics would always coincide with those of Sartre.[9]

The energetic Francophilia of many people writing about Beauvoir, which includes an extraordinarily selective view of her France that often fails to recognize both the particularity of her own life and the larger world of France outside Paris, has arguably done something of a disservice to women, as distinct from feminist theory. The passion, the voice of authoritative assertion and the fierce coherence of *The Second Sex* also often implicitly made women both victims (as the 'other' of all discourse or the person who is not the fully human subject) and endlessly, and in different ways, an imperfect model of the human.[10] The various human forms which women might take (daughter, lover, mother and so on) are implicitly forms of failure in which women do not achieve selfhood. It is not that the men that Beauvoir presents (or cites in her extremely partial view of world literature) are themselves models of what humanity might be, but at least they are able, in her view, to act freely. Margaret Walters has written of the way in which Beauvoir wishes women to claim male selfhood, but with little regard for what that selfhood might involve or the way in which it is at least as unstable, contradictory and flawed as that of women.[11] It is not that Beauvoir follows Professor Higgins in the musical *My Fair Lady* in asking why a woman cannot be more like a man, but that she does not ask those questions about masculinity which have now become commonplace amongst not just feminists but to anyone writing about norms of sexuality. Equally, what Beauvoir does in her writing about women and men is, arguably, to reinforce the form of subjectivity which men inhabit and suggest that the only defence and way forward for women is through an adoption of that very position.

But the questioning of this problematic nature of any stereotype of gender does not emerge in feminism until there had occurred that much wider recognition and use of psychoanalytic theory which took place from the late 1970s onwards. In what can be seen as the second period of feminism's engagement with the modern – one in which psychoanalysis became intellectually significant, and in which the politics of gay liberation initiated a radical rethinking of global understandings of masculinity – that binary of *The Second Sex* began to be more problematic.[12] Prior to that, Beauvoir's *The Second Sex* had inspired authors such as Shulamith Firestone (in *The Dialectic of Sex*) and had clearly been a formative influence on Kate Millett (in *Sexual Politics*), together with other writers in the tradition which became known as radical feminism.[13] What is interesting here is that numbers of feminists have consistently been able to take from Beauvoir her sexual politics (that is, to work with a binary division between women and men) but to abandon her left-wing politics more or less entirely. Those politics began to emerge in a more public form after the Second World War, through her association with Sartre and others in part, but also, towards the end of her life, with the French feminism of the 1970s. Beauvoir 'came out' as a feminist and took part in openly feminist demonstrations in that decade, but in two crucial ways she still remained loyal to her own account of sexuality and gender politics. Indeed, when writing about the reception of *The Second Sex*, Beauvoir had noted that she was happy to have avoided 'the trap of feminism', a hugely interesting and significant phrase which still demands attention, not just in terms of Beauvoir's perception of her own work but in terms of what she implies about the dangers of the divorce of feminist concerns from other forms of politics.[14]

So for those who wish to associate feminism with radical differences of subjectivity between women and men, there is little comfort in Beauvoir's work, for she consistently refused to entertain the idea that there were such differences. Thus, whilst writing throughout *The Second Sex* of very fixed categories of women and men (and largely the construction of the identity of the category of 'woman' by reference to that of men and masculinity), she did not endorse the work of her compatriots (although not her contemporaries) who were proposing other forms of difference between women and men. The work of the French feminists Luce Irigaray and Monique Wittiq, for example, remained consistently alien to Beauvoir.[15] The second aspect of *The Second Sex* that came to separate it from much feminist work from the 1970s onwards is that Beauvoir never abandoned her critique of psychoanalysis, a form of practice that does, centrally, involve self-critique and self-examination, as well as an acceptance of the theory of the unconscious. For a committed rationalist such as Beauvoir, that idea must have been tantamount to an assault on her most cherished beliefs about the place of the thinking subject in the world.

So whilst Beauvoir was fully prepared to recognize (and appreciate) the changes that had taken place in France between her own childhood and that of young women in France of the 1960s and the 1970s, she remained committed to that category of the 'rational' which psychoanalytically informed and cross-culturally aware feminists began to make problematic from the 1980s onwards. This form of feminism made connections between a social context and the ideas it generated, and invested no idea with absolute authority or absolute autonomy. In this, feminism in part tacitly endorsed the connections that Marx had initiated (and which later generations of scholars educated in Marxism, such as Walter Benjamin, were to explore) between circumstance and culture; to repeat Marx's pithy comment: 'Men make their own history, but they do not make it just as they please; they do not make it under circumstances chosen by themselves, but under circumstances directly encountered and transmitted from the past. The tradition of all the dead generations weighs like a nightmare on the brain of the living.'[16] But what happened to this idea was that it often led feminists in two directions: to the connection of certain kinds of gender-specific practices (of which veiling and female genital mutilation were the most often discussed) as forms of 'the past', and to assumptions about the implicit emancipation of those societies which had abandoned these practices. Walter Benjamin was to write in 1940, in his essay 'Theses on the Philosophy of History', of 'the Angel of History', a person who is about to be overtaken by the horrors of 'progress'.[17] Benjamin himself was about to die as result of the horrors of the Second World War, but the wider point of this work is to point to the ways in which, as much as any society might wish to repair its fractures and deficiencies (in this context, forms of gender inequality), it is nevertheless constantly being propelled towards further and even more disturbing possibilities.

None of the political problems for feminism that are implicit in postmodernism (or other, even more exaggerated definitions of current politics, such as the 'post-political') are derived directly from Beauvoir. But the reason why the long-term impact of her book remains so important is twofold: first, it supports a theory of social transformation that is situated in discourse; the view that if we transform the way in which a culture thinks about women, then the culture – and the world – will be transformed; and second, it maintains an expectation of human 'progress', in which the problems of the past have not been solved but form what might be described as a redundant historical space. Beauvoir (like Judith Butler) was educated in philosophy, a discipline which, whilst complex and abstract, has a long tradition of writing the human condition as male. It is not that what is said is not, and was not, relevant to women, but it does not constitute the entirety of human experience. Beauvoir's greatness lies in the way in which she initiated the possibility of seeing the implications of biological difference. For all that, for some years after the publication of *The Second Sex* the implications of the book were seldom discussed; no significant secondary literature exists on Beauvoir until the 1970s, and although the book was a best-seller when first published, little was done in the decade immediately following its publication to work through – or with – its implications. Neither, it has to be said, was there much discussion of other works about women published at about the same time, for instance Viola Klein's *The Feminine Character: History of an Ideology* (first published in 1946), which had a different understanding of the dynamics of social change as well as the origins of gender stereotypes than *The Second Sex*.[18] It was an understanding that was to be further articulated by Klein in the book that she published in 1956 with Alva Myrdal entitled *Women's Two Roles: Home and Work*.[19]

Changing Times

Klein and Beauvoir had both, in different ways and in the light of very different traditions, raised the question of the place of women in the post-1945 world. Nevertheless, the question was largely shelved by writers of non-fiction throughout the 1950s, and it was not until the publication of Betty Friedan's *The Feminine Mystique* in 1963 that the 'woman question' again became a matter of international debate. What is interesting here – as has been the case in other instances where certain kinds of radical change or radical rethinking of the conventional world have occurred – is that fiction had identified many of the themes of Friedan's work before that book was published. To return to three novels already mentioned: Sylvia Plath's *The Bell Jar*, published in 1963, Evan Connell's *Mrs Bridge*, published in 1959, and Richard Yates's *Revolutionary Road*, published in 1961. All these authors wrote of the personal misery of women's lives in the suburbs of the United States, the tortuous evasions and deceits around questions of sexuality, and above all the absence of any escape from powerful demands for conformity in these locations of what was supposed to be the 'American dream'. Friedan's book shares much of the sense of the isolation and unhappiness of the women locked into this world, whilst at the same time it is a powerful denunciation of a society's refusal of women's right to a place in the public world. Couched in terms of the lives of white, middle-class graduates, Friedan's book had a degree of eventual irrelevance in the sense that the world she wrote about would not remain immediately interesting to subsequent generations schooled in the feminist politics of class and race, but it had a very important place in terms of the contribution that it made to the feminism of the United States. Betty Friedan herself became a founder member of the National Organization for Women (NOW), which campaigned about, amongst other issues, the passing of Equal Rights legislation in the United States.[20] Many of the aspirations and expectations (both of what should be changed and what did not need changing) of NOW informed the feminism that was to become the organizing force of the movement that was exported, through institutions such as the United Nations and the World Bank, to the global south. That movement put, as feminism had done since the days of Mary Wollstonecraft, a premium on the education of women, assuming that this would transform gender relations and that 'education' – with all its problematic diversity and inevitable contribution not just to social emancipation but also to forms of social hierarchy – would in itself be a transformative agenda. What can be detected at work is again a narrative of reassurance: that this focus of feminism will enhance rather than undermine the status quo.

In terms of the history of feminism, it is also striking that Friedan's book emerged in a context where the 'woman question' was *already* an issue in the public politics of the United States. Indeed, the impetus to a public discussion of women's rights had been put on the public agenda of the United States by the establishment in 1961 by the Kennedy administration of a National Commission on Women. In 1964 this was followed by the passing of the Civil Rights Act by the Johnson administration, which made various forms of discrimination – including that of sex – illegal. The times which were a-changing, as Bob Dylan sang in 1964, were times of very powerful challenges in various contexts, not least that of an increasingly diverse and globally informed *aesthetic* of gender.

To consider the changes in gender relations that took place throughout much of the global north during the 1960s and 1970s in terms of an aesthetic is to emphasize the way in which various forms of dissent in these decades were focused on the body and its appearance. The young people who were seen in the international media at music festivals – most famously Woodstock's 'three days of peace and music' in 1969 – quite simply looked like a different generation. Long-haired, scantily clothed in public, unashamed of unregulated forms of sexuality, these young people provoked sclerotic reactions in some whilst being welcomed enthusiastically by others. Not least among the latter were those various entrepreneurial interests which foresaw the profits to be made out of a more publicly expressed sexuality. The naked body, whether male or female, could now be seen in human form, outside the static examples of art galleries, whilst it could also be spoken of more openly. When, at the trial in London in 1960 about the publication of D.H. Lawrence's *Lady Chatterley's Lover*, the prosecuting counsel, Mervyn Griffith-Jones, spoke of the wives and servants who he suggested should not read the book, he clearly did not realize that as well as speaking of categories who were rapidly disappearing (at least in terms of their own sense of identity), he was also speaking of a social world increasingly unsegregated by gender. This was itself part of a shifting urban aesthetic: as more women became part of the workforce, the towns and cities in which people of the global north lived and worked became increasingly used by both women and men. No longer did those suburbs which Friedan berated so fiercely constitute the only appropriate 'place' for women. As women moved into the cities, marches by women to 'reclaim' the night took place throughout the last decades of the twentieth century; at stake was the centrally important idea that public urban space should be open to all.

Nor was it only public, urban space which became the focus of feminist campaigns in the late twentieth century. Previously all-male segregated professional and social spaces (from the ordination of women in the Church of England to the opening of golf clubs to women members) became the focus of re-energized feminist campaigns. Nor, importantly, was resistance to the access of women to these spaces always confined to one political party; across the global north, people of many political persuasions spoke for the ending of what were increasingly seen as 'old-fashioned' assumptions and practices. The invocation of fashion, as a cluster of aspirations and the inspiration of a major global industry, started to pose all kinds of questions for politicians and voters alike: the question of what should be retained in terms of social norms and what should, like last year's clothes, be abandoned. The nostalgia for the past (and generally an entirely fictitious past) that clearly exists has been the subject of much academic attention; in the UK, Raphael Samuel and other historians associated with the History Workshop group have been outstanding contributors to this work.[21] Yet as cultures across the world become increasingly informed, if not invaded, by values and aspirations shaped largely in the global north, the question of the gender of tradition becomes increasingly important, not least because in certain contexts resistance to what are seen as 'western' values about gender are pivotal to furious and often bloody attacks on the west. Dress codes that implicitly assume the responsibility of women for the sexual continence of men are policed and defended with energy, and the social segregation of women and men is maintained, as are the very different forms of access to education that women and men are allowed. Forms of gender segregation that might once have been central only to a social elite are generalized for an entire society. For example, countries such as Turkey, once determined to situate themselves as 'modern' in terms of their abandonment of traditional forms of dress for women, rediscover an enthusiasm for those expectations about women which had once been consigned to history.[22]

In the hardening of these lines of gender segregation, the global north has much to answer for, not least because its own record on gender equality has been so often limited and so little relevant to any except the most privileged. But part of the complexity of the emerging aesthetic of gender, which has been part of global representations of gender since the mid-1970s, is that accompanying some of the emancipatory possibilities of this aesthetic is a very much more problematic issue about the commercial exploitation of fantasies about the body. As most citizens of the global north might praise a greater social openness about the body, its complaints and its possibilities, there has also been a parallel emergence of commodified representations of the body, and generally the female body, which perpetuate forms of the male control of women, not the least of which is the possibility of financial gain. Instances of these gains are the sexualization of all kinds of everyday commodities and experiences, from children's clothing (the infamous slogan on a child's T-shirt 'So Many Boys, So Little Time') to advertising on aeroplanes ('Fly a Younger Fleet'). That last slogan appears (or used to appear) on some of Richard Branson's Virgin planes: a company which from its start has used sexual innuendo in order to sell goods and services. What might have appeared initially as a completely random branding exercise in the association of selling recorded music and train tickets with the word 'Virgin' can now be seen as a determined exercise in the sexualization of everyday purchases.

However, Branson's endlessly priapic commercial policies are just one example of that close synergy between advertising copy and implicit sexual reference which has been noted since the early twentieth century. At least as important in terms of questions about gender inequality are the ways in which global communication, and in particular the explosion of individual access to its various forms (Twitter and Facebook being the most widely used examples), has facilitated the contexts for all kinds of misogyny and abuse about women. This feature of the twenty-first century has much extended those debates about censorship which – in the 1980s – were so divisive for feminism. When Andrea Dworkin and Catharine MacKinnon emerged as passionate critics of the various forms of pornography, they were writing largely about a print and film culture.[23] Their work was the subject of attack from those feminists who were concerned about the consequences of censorship, in particular the questions of who would be the censors and exactly what was to be censored. Given the very long record in the west of battles about censorship (from vernacular versions of the Bible in the sixteenth century to the case of *Lady Chatterley's Lover* to attacks on books about evolution), this was an entirely understandable concern.

But few in the late twentieth century can have had any idea of the eventual global range of the evolving new forms of communication and the powerful and misogynist homogeneity of much of their content. This homogeneity has taken the form of both literal representations of women (the dominance of the slim, white, young woman) and expressions about the proper behaviour of women, 'proper' often being defined in terms of acquiescence in the dominant order of gender. As various women who have chosen to 'speak feminism' – for example Caroline Criado-Perez – have found, speaking feminism attracts extreme forms of insult and threat. In the case of Criado-Perez, the threat of a picture of Jane Austen (often, if falsely, interpreted as the very epitome of English conservatism) on English banknotes was enough to provoke threats of rape and death.[24] It is not that women do not speak back and/or attack their critics (and there are now many important feminist blogs) but that there continues a persistent sense amongst some men, often fuelled by patriarchal interpretations of religion, that theirs is the right to assert, and to assert with the full confidence that they speak with generally sanctioned legitimacy. This problematic right to 'rule giving', which is an aspect of male behaviour that goes back as far as Moses, is one that constantly engages women in a defensive position. The agenda of gender is thus too often set in terms of male interests, interests which are assumed to represent humanity in general. Moreover, women themselves have often appeared to be unaware of the extent to which women have been written out of history. For example, if we examine a book written in 1896 by Frances Buss, a woman always described as a 'feminist' pioneer in terms of the education of young women, what we find is an extraordinary use of the term 'we'. In the collected advice to her young female pupils, Buss writes frequently of the rights that 'we' have. At the time of the book's publication, when British women had no right to vote or access to formal political representation, one of the rights that Buss is so eager to communicate to her pupils is that of the various virtues of the British political system, in which 'we' have the right to vote. That inclusive 'we' is of course exclusive, and extraordinary in the light of contemporary feminist campaigns.[25]

Feminism faces, as it has always faced, the problem of how it is to intervene in the social world and what the term 'feminism' might mean across the world. But it does so in the context of what can be described as a third phase of the engagement of feminism with the modern, in which it has to encounter a truly global culture and new kinds of complexities in the loyalties of individuals to both their own and imported cultures. In this context, it is useful to look back at feminism and attempt to define those consistencies in it, the moments of the most inclusive feminist politics, as well as those moments when there is considerable dissent and disagreement. In terms of global history, there would seem to be two themes which more than others have united women in various forms of feminist campaigns. One has been the demand for women to have the same degree of control over their person as that of men: rights to the same civic status and to autonomy as an individual. This would appear to be, at least in terms of the law and/or written constitutions, a relatively straightforward matter to achieve, a matter of ensuring gender neutrality in the letter of the law. But of course achieving this has been very far from simple and is still resisted in many countries. Nor is it necessarily only resisted by men; as was the case in campaigns on suffrage and divorce in Britain, there were, and are, important minorities of women who do not support more inclusive policies. Although it is now widely suggested, in terms of both the United States and Britain, that women are more likely to vote for left-of-centre political parties than men are, a glance at the literature on voting in both countries shows that this was not always the case and that, for example, throughout the 1950s in Britain, women were identified as more likely to vote for the Conservative rather than for the Labour Party.[26] This in itself is perhaps not surprising, since it is supposed that the public culture of Britain in the 1950s, in common with that of the United States, was one which was far from radical in its gendered assumptions. But, as various authors have pointed out, what may have appeared as the settled conservatism of the 1950s hid important currents of dissatisfaction and make the appearance of a new form of femininity in the 1960s less surprising.[27] This new form of woman no longer appears in advertisements in a rapturous relationship with her kitchen but is now expressing a more than active interest in the world outside. This returns us to the importance of that transformation of the aesthetic of gender in the 1960s and the 1970s: the emergence of the happy young woman who was famously portrayed as 'having come a long way'.[28]

This takes us to the question – central to feminism – of who the female person is who is both the subject and the object of feminist campaigns. The hostile, critical view of feminism and 'the feminist' has a long history of relating commitment to feminism with disruptive and disenchanted women: the woman who wishes to wreak havoc on the world because it has failed to reward her in various ways. The 2014 western campaign of 'This is what a feminist looks like' was a very explicit challenge to this attitude, the message being that feminism comes in all genders, races, ages and every other aspect of physical appearance.[29] But the very necessity of this campaign suggests the depth, the range and power of the idea that feminism is somehow the location of a particular form of female failure: that of attracting male approval. Yet although the question of attracting (or not attracting) male approval can take an explicitly sexual form, it is also a foundational part of the gender dynamics of those institutional spheres in which women have long demanded inclusion – politics and education – and nevertheless remain significantly unequal. No political or educational system in any part of the world has ever been gender neutral; some remain determinedly the sphere only of the biologically male. In the context of education, for example, any absolute bar on the education of women is widely condemned, yet many responsible for that condemnation forget that formal access to education is only the beginning of an individual's educational career. The extent to which education is continued beyond basic literacy, and how gender inequalities are reproduced within education as much as outside of it, remain crucial issues, one of the most important being the extent to which women within educational institutions conform to male expectations, and do so in order to receive forms of approval derived from the masculine.[30]

The example of gender inequalities in education presents us with an important context in which to consider the history of the interplay of educational reforms and gender. In historical terms, and across much of the world, there is evidence that until the nineteenth century very few women, as well as very few men, had any extended education. Levels of literacy, for example, only began to rise in the global north in the twentieth century, and although literacy has now become much more general throughout the world, for millions of people education beyond primary levels is limited. The emphasis here should be on 'people', since for once the word, which in other contexts wilfully or otherwise obscures differences of gender, in this case does relate to widely shared experiences of women and men. If we take both Britain and the United States as examples of countries where mass, free education was introduced in the second half of the nineteenth century, there were few effective protests about educating white women as well as white men, and the term 'children' had a force which transcended questions of gender. Boys and girls were often taught different subjects, in different ways, but it was recognized that all children should be in some form of education. The most heated protests, and this was crucially important in the United States, were about access to education for black people, a form of discrimination which was to be reproduced in the twentieth century in apartheid-era South Africa. Differences of race had less formal impact on the history of state education in Britain than class. But if we look at one of the most famous suffragette posters, white working-class men – who are all able to vote – are set against the clearly middle-class, but voteless, female.[31] This is an argument for the enfranchisement of women that, yet again, draws on the tradition of moral economy within feminism in which 'good' women ardently wish to play their part in social betterment. So powerful is this tradition that in the early 1950s the politician Adlai Stevenson was able to tell a graduating class at Smith College, an elite women's college in the United States, that education for women was an important contribution to the happiness of husbands.

Congratulations to an assembly of women graduates for having spent four, probably hard-working, years in college in order to ensure better-informed conversation with a husband over the dinner table is unlikely to occur today. But what is likely to occur is that graduating classes will be told two things: first of all that higher education is only the beginning of adult life, and second that education is of benefit to a larger society. For many people these commonly reproduced clichés would be unremarkable, nor would many people remark that in the world outside the academy (itself a place far from free of various forms of discrimination) graduates will encounter a highly gendered labour market. In that life outside the academy, the women graduates will find that their achievements are rewarded less well than those of their male fellow students, and that fifteen years after graduation the differences in those rewards will have become more distinct. What is being reproduced in these silences about the differences for women and men in life after university is what Joan Scott has called the 'fantasy' of feminist history, a fantasy which remains blind to changing material circumstances and yet assumes a steady 'progress' to gender equality against consistent male opposition.[32] However, a study of the history of women's access to education in the global north demonstrates that privileged women have always had some access to some forms of education, and that throughout the twentieth century various forms of the democratization of educational access were achieved, with very few voices suggesting that women should be absolutely excluded from this process. It is true that some exceptionally privileged institutions (the cases of the universities of Oxford and Cambridge are particularly notable here) did not hurry to open their doors to women, but in the same historical period other universities (or university colleges) did so. What this account of the history of higher education interrupts is the comfortable belief in a coherent, considered and determined resistance to the higher education of women. This fantasy is then related to a more general account of social life which assumes an unbroken and unchallenged refusal of education to women, as well as supporting an account of history in which men and male institutions consistently resisted the education, higher or otherwise, of women. Those nineteenth-century writers (quoted in the work of Jeffrey Weeks) who suggested that educated women would become mentally disturbed, if not also infertile, were met with derision, not just in the twenty-first century but also at the time that they were writing.[33]

Rather than explicit and determined sexist exclusion, what the history of education in the global north suggests is a pattern of the gendered accommodation of various institutions to changing norms and material needs. Most obviously, for example, as nineteenth-century Britain became, in some areas of the country, both more industrialized and more urban, so there emerged new forms of infrastructure (particularly what became known in the twentieth century as the 'service' sector) which provided employment for women. But it was not just that employment was available, but also that this employment had certain needs of its employees: that they should be literate and socialized in appropriate ways. This suggests that the history of the employment of women in paid work, like that of education, is one in which a reading which suggests constant resistance to the presence of women obscures a different pattern: that as the economy changed, so expectations of gender changed.

Unchanging Times

One of the implications of this reading of the past two hundred years (and indeed of the present) is that just as much as women have often been welcomed into the service of various forms of political economies (be they those of capitalism or socialism), the focus of resistance to the presence and the interests of women has, consistently, been that of the refusal of public power to women. It is here that accommodative change and various forms of apparently 'progressive' welcome to the employment and the education of women are stalled. It is also centrally related to the way in which feminism – again across cultures and history – has turned to legislative change in order to secure greater access for women to power, in terms of the chance both to exercise it and to influence the agenda of the powerful. 'Going to law' has become a major plank of feminist causes since the nineteenth century, and as the world globalized, so a place for global law about gender equality has emerged and has become central to organizations such as the United Nations.

By the end of the first decade of the twenty-first century, feminists throughout the world could look back on fifty years in which there had been numerous changes to the legal status of women. In 1970, for example, married women in England could not sign a hire purchase agreement without their husband's consent, and there remained important differences between what were then described as legitimate and illegitimate children. But in looking back at the histories of the change in the related legislation, it is important to ask two questions that are central to feminism: first, the extent to which ideas very specifically related to feminism were responsible for the changes, and second, the degree to which the changes were part of general changes in the attitudes and the expectations of people in the global north, many of which had little specifically to do with feminism (and were not derived from it) but had a great deal to do with other changing material and ideological circumstances. This is not about refusing the part that feminism played in contributing to these circumstances, but it is about, for example, the way in which by the 1970s it was becoming increasingly obvious, in the west, that economies based on consumer spending could not be maintained without both the full participation of all adults and the relaxation of many of those norms which had once been regarded as central to social order. Popular culture played its part, as it had always done, in allowing irreverence and refusal of aspects of the social status quo, but now those forms were brought to mass audiences. When John Lennon remarked that the Beatles were now more famous than Jesus Christ, he very economically summed up this transition: whilst a tradition of satire had existed in the modern world from the days of Hogarth, technology was making that tradition generally available, across place, gender and degree of education.

In this evolving order – an order which was to continue to change and is still changing rather than being a static form – what was to become clearer in the last decades of the twentieth century was that, as aspects of social life became more androgynous (for example, in terms of institutional access and legal position), so sites of power began to change, not least the growing subservience of national politics to the interests of international capital. Whilst western states allowed (if in some cases with great and persisting unwillingness and opposition) all kinds of legislative change around questions of sexuality, what also occurred was a gradual internationalization of economic agendas. At the same time 'Reaganomics', as this was first called after the economic theory that prevailed when Ronald Reagan was president of the USA, preached the virtues of the small state These views were challenged in some quarters but gradually hardened into the dominance of neoliberal certainties in the twenty-first century. The problem of this transition for feminist politics is considerable, since it demands first and foremost a coming to terms with the realities of the sheer scale and distance of contemporary forms of power. The British House of Commons which, in the first decade of the twentieth century, resisted giving women the vote was an institution made up of about six hundred men, all of whom – as remains the case – could be named (if not shamed); it was visible, human power, entirely unlike that of those who direct international companies. Investigative writers and journalists, such as Owen Jones, Naomi Klein and Michael Moore, have unpicked some of the human connections of power, but any social movement – from Occupy to feminism – which wishes to challenge the interests of contemporary power has to confront the difficulties of finding a sure focus.[34] Inevitably, this sense of the distance of power does not only empower the radicalism of the left; it is also a major cause of the radicalism of the right. Emboldened by that sense of the 'little person' (the important person in the rise of German fascism, as the artist George Grosz and others pointed out) who has been betrayed and ignored by politicians, there are political movements throughout not just Europe but the world which attempt to revive the politics of what is literally familiar or familiar only through fantasy.[35]

The sense of 'distance' between the political class and the rest of the world thus has the consequence of creating a space in which various kinds of fantasies, including those which concern gender and gender relations, can inhabit that vacuum created by disengagement with formal and institutional politics. For many people, politicians of major, formal parties are a distant, and inevitably corrupt, group. In this context, the question, very much for feminism as for other campaigning groups, is where political activity might be located and directed. It is apparent that throughout much of the contemporary world there are two forms of political energy. The first is that of the demand for greater and more engaged forms of democracy, and particularly for forms of politics that engage with questions of corporate power and its hold on political agendas and decisions. The second is that of discontent: a discontent with aspects of change (gay marriage, the greater public visibility and agency of women, and encroachment on national boundaries) that seem to threaten achieved national and personal identities. Both these forms of political energy have found ways of expressing their views through what is, literally, the World Wide Web.

That web is often the site of extreme forms of misogyny – for instance, on various national and international versions of the British *Daily Mail*'s so-called 'Sidebar of Shame'. These sites, like others in the popular press, are often organized around the policing of women's bodies and sexuality, with an undercurrent of concern about same-sex relationships. The readership of these sites is considerable and as such they represent a tsunami of debased, and debasing, comments, largely (although not exclusively) about

women. The problem here is that of challenge; of how to inter-
rupt this poisonous flow of material, particularly because, as Sara
Ahmed has pointed out, the person called 'the feminist' is often
constructed as the spoilsport, the person who breaks up the party,
the humourless harridan who is against 'fun' – the same form of
'fun' which, as Lauren Berlant and Arlie Hochschild have shown,
dooms us to the greatest disappointment.[36] Given that there are
considerable industries – and a great deal of money – that depend
upon 'fun', it is all too easy for any opposition to this often implicitly and explicitly misogynist culture to be marginalized, and to be
marginalized as 'just feminist', or as that other contemporary form
of challenge to privilege which is dubbed 'politically correct'. The
institutions and the interests that control the output of this material, material which combines legitimate 'fun' with forms of sexism
and homophobia, are more than able to turn criticism into the
reinforcement of the views being put forward.

So the possibilities for feminist resistance to the many ways in
which women are stereotyped, trivialized, debased and ignored
in the mass media are often framed within those discourses which
assume the legitimate dominance of a 'male' or patriarchal culture.
The critique of this tradition has a long, and distinguished, tradition
in feminist writing (including figures such as Wollstonecraft and
Beauvoir) and among other women – novelists and artists – who
have recorded the often painful costs of being female. Amongst this
tradition are figures such as the great women artists of the twentieth century: Louise Bourgeois, Hannah Höch, Barbara Hepworth
and Käthe Kollwitz, and more recently Ellen Gallagher. The collective strength of this tradition is a hugely vivid challenge to the
idea that male biology constitutes either the definitive human form
or the only form of moral and intellectual legitimacy. But having
said that, what remain are troubling questions and issues about
the interpretation of cultural traditions as singly and solely about
the authority of one gender. To assume, as feminist writers of the
1970s often did, that misogyny was the only worthwhile enemy in
town overlooks two things: most obviously the other social processes, most particularly of class and race, through which privilege
is maintained, and perhaps less obviously that tradition of satire,
irreverence, subversion and transgression which has always been

suspicious of authority, and mocking of its various forms, not least masculinity.

This second tradition is not, of course, recorded with the same reverence as the work of Michelangelo or the novels of Tolstoy, but it is closely linked to the first tradition, not least because one of the most powerful definitions of any great art (whatever its form) is that it disturbs and engages our critical attention. Yet those two ideas (of the disturbance of the taken-for-granted by great art and of the rich seams of irreverence in many societies) have had to face complex and often contradictory changes in the definition and organization of culture, all of which have implications for feminism and feminists. What we can observe of the years since the mid-1980s is the recognition of previously ignored women artists and writers, whilst conventional locations and subjects of art have been disturbed by technological innovations and the acceptance of the fluid boundaries between 'great', canonical traditions and the popular. Both these changes have contributed to the enlargement of our ideas about what is 'culture', combined with the growth of various forms of communication, to a much wider and more generally available space for the discussion of ideas. But with that has gone the ever-more powerful authority of markets and genres of 'culture' manufactured, like the Spice Girls, for specific markets. Thus the apparently enlarged space of 'culture' arrives with the rigidly defined limits and expectations of other forms of the market, with their often marginalizing effect. In this, we might come to see that we have to be more careful in making confident assertions about the patriarchal past of culture, and its replacement by cultures that are more inclusive in terms of gender differences.

One of the many great achievements of late twentieth-century feminist scholarship was, perhaps paradoxically, to challenge that reading of the past which assumes a landscape dominated by patriarchal authority. As scholars such as Eve Sedgwick have demonstrated, gender has always been an unstable, but constant, constituent of the imagination, be it collective or individual.[37] Various forms of institutional life have been quite clearly dominated by, and only accessible to, men, but the importance of these institutional barriers has to be seen in terms of their lasting significance as well as that of participation. For example, to assume that women were excluded in nineteenth-century England from intellectual life, and only achieved access to it through the opening up of the universities, obscures a number of important issues, not least the view that intellectual life is dependent upon universities. It also obscures the socially functional derivation of changes in policies about all forms of education across Europe and North America in the nineteenth century, and across much of the rest of the world in the twentieth. Amongst these changes were those of an increasingly urban society, dependent on technological skill and an infrastructure which could support and distribute the products of new forms of production. To accept as unproblematic the view that women have always had to battle for changes in the institutional world is a rhetoric which, whilst it empowers statements about female solidarity and the sense of a shared and combative past, can also have the effect of prolonging gender inequality, because of the refusal of the rhetoric to address the overall structural complexities of inequality and the equally complex processes which both inhibit and encourage change. Hence what is important is that we recognize the multiple meanings and causes in changes in the situation of women: to read, for instance, the employment of women in various forms of the new service industries of the late nineteenth-century west as an unambiguous form of emancipation is to obscure the ways in which that employment served the interests of capital and enabled the extension of consumer markets. The various consequences of this change cannot simply be read as 'emancipation', although that may have been one of the aspects of the change.

Questions about how we might challenge gender inequality in the twenty-first century form part of the following chapter, but there are some important concluding comments to be made here about the ways in which feminism has engaged – and is engaging – with gendered inequality. The first is that structural accounts of gendered inequality, accounts which engage with the intersection of class, race and gendered inequality, have had something of a less than entirely enthusiastic reception in some feminist quarters. This problematic relationship has been discussed since the nineteenth century. Here, in Rachel Holmes's 2014 biography of Eleanor Marx, we have a summary of the views of Eleanor:

Eleanor always supported the campaigns for women's suffrage and rights-based arguments but knew that their application was politically limited: creating access to the ballot box and education for bourgeois women was a partial intervention that would not address the broad underlying structural problem of sexual inequality . . . women should be forming a united feminist front, challenging across class divisions the divide and rule that regulates production and reproduction.[38]

And here is Eleanor Marx in her own words:

Here comes the struggle against man. Here the educated woman – the doctor, the clerk, the lawyer, is the antagonist of man. The women of this class are sick of their moral and intellectual subjugation . . . the working woman cannot be like the bourgeois woman who has to fight against the man of her own class . . . The objections of the bourgeois man to the rights of women are only a matter of competition . . . With the proletarian women, on the contrary, it is a struggle of the woman with the man of her own class against the capitalist class.[39]

These questions of class were central to the disputes within the British campaign for suffrage. In her biography of Sylvia Pankhurst, Katherine Connolly has shown how in that famous family of suffrage, the Pankhursts, there were very different ways of looking at the social world and the people within it. Connolly cites an exchange between two of the Pankhurst sisters, Christabel and Sylvia, in which Christabel argues that the lives of working-class women are too hard and 'their education too meagre to equip them for the contest'. Christabel's description of the lives of working-class women in Britain at the beginning of the twentieth century was correct but what she made of this was more problematic. This was her argument: 'We want picked women, the very strongest and most intelligent.'[40]

This aside about the consequences of the mechanics of social reproduction has a close relationship to feminism and to the ways in which certain aspects of feminism have engaged in the social world. Not the least of those ways, and the second question about feminism which is to be discussed here, is that of feminism in the academy, the academic feminism that has blossomed across the

world since the 1970s. This was a result of the refusal of much
of the curriculum of higher education up to that point to recognize that human beings came in two different biological forms,
and that, through the complexities of gendered practices, there
emerged quite considerable differences between the lives of, to
put it in its simplest form, women and men. The anthropology
textbook which included the sentence 'everybody has a father
and a mother, most have siblings, most have wives and children'
summed up the view of many in the academic world; 'people'
were male.[41] It was not, as the work discussed previously here by
Viola Klein and Simone de Beauvoir illustrated, that women were
not present in – or close to, in the case of Beauvoir – the august
halls of academe. But it was a minority presence in terms of human
beings, and arguably even more of a minority presence in terms of
the discussion and the recognition of the implications of gender
difference. An explosion in this peaceful scene of misogyny came
when universities themselves expanded their intake and in doing
so admitted not just more students but more female students, many
of whom took one look at the curriculum of the humanities and
the social sciences and decided – rightly – that this had nothing to
do with them.

Thus, across the west, institutions of knowledge and communication had to confront two very powerful feminist arguments:
first, the way in which that very 'higher learning' on which the
west so prided itself was seriously lacking in its recognition of the
world as a whole, and second, that this context – publicly committed as it was supposed to be to open debate and democratic
discussion – was in many ways a fierce defender of social and gendered power. Of all the battles that feminism fought in the 1970s
and 1980s, the rewriting of the syllabi of the academy was amongst
the most successful. New histories were discovered and with them
new, female, inhabitants of the past; taken-for-granted assumptions
about the world were shattered, not least the assumption that the
west had secured the emancipation of women. New connections
were made between the academy and the worlds of government
policy: in the UK the argument was made for the recognition
of those who spent their (entirely unrewarded) lives caring for
others.[42] Cases were made in the academy about the ways in which

the law gave priority to the interests of men, and across much of the west there were notable victories, often formed and generated in universities, which changed the relationship of women to both the practice and the letter of the law.[43]

These changes and struggles gave to the 1970s a sense of that 'bliss to be alive' which had not always been characteristic of academic life. Yet contemporary voices expressed concern about the location and to a certain extent the containment of feminist energy within the academy. The word 'academization' began to be heard, and with it a critique of those in the academy whose feminist work constituted precisely that kind of career-building exercise – those theoretical revolutions of which Thomas Kuhn wrote so persuasively – which had long been a feature of academic lives.[44] These accusations failed to recognize the way in which much innovative academic work is not always rewarded with notice: the extent to which feminist ideas in the academy have been rewarded has been the subject of much discussion, but the accusations that feminist academic work is motivated solely by opportunistic motives obscures two aspects of the question. The first is, as already suggested, that all academic systems of knowledge can only maintain their vitality through the integration of new ideas. Indeed, the academy would come to resemble a very empty shell if it remained rooted in the reiteration of traditional views and perspectives. The second aspect of this question which is important is the very real fact that what is said and taught in universities matters. It may not have the immediate impact of ideas made in the wider world, but it is wrong to say that academic feminism (or other ideas critical of the political status quo) is somehow an obscure exercise in the manipulation of irrelevant debates. In both the UK and the USA, feminist scholarship has informed changes in the law and various kinds of public practice. Even if feminist scholarship can on occasions tend towards the incomprehensible end of the continuum of forms of human communication, it is more generally the case that much feminist academic work is immediately and generally accessible. Importantly too, what feminism achieved in the academy is the integration of what might once have been described as 'everyday' life, the study of quotidian existence often deemed too 'trivial' for serious academic attention. For example, feminist scholarship, in the work of writers such as Ann Oakley, and before her Hannah Gavron, brought into the mainstream of social science research the study of childbirth and of housework.[45] With this came two other important shifts. The first was the idea that the relationship between the researcher and the researched should not be taken for granted, but that the implicit power relations within that exchange have to be recognized. The second was the recognition that the choice and the direction of the subjects of academic attention are closely related to the interests of forms of power: to disturb the mechanisms of that connection has been a very important theme of feminist work, which has continued the traditions of the work of people such as C.W. Mills and Marie Jahoda.[46]

It is more than likely that debates about the contribution of academic feminism to feminist politics will continue for some time, as will the energy and the application of feminist scholarship. That scholarship will take place in universities which have become central to a globalized world, in that they provide recognizable credentials and assist in the making of an increasingly invasive and often neoliberal Anglophone culture. But at the same time there is also a sense in which feminist arguments within universities, precisely because they inevitably take place within specialized academic discourses and practices, are if not superseded then at least accompanied by debates and organizing on the web. These new forms can accommodate the fast-moving immediacy of many political events, and are vastly more accessible than participation in academic debates. Individuals can now communicate their views about all aspects of gender relations to hitherto unknown numbers of people: an aspect of twenty-first-century technology which provides – and will no doubt continue to provide – rather different challenges from those associated with the exchange of academic views.

One of the many women who have written about the challenges and the negative implication of this new world is the British writer Laurie Penny. In a 2014 book – published in the entirely traditional way by a print-and-paper technology – she writes of the initial expectations of the web:

> There was a time, not so long ago, when nerds, theorists and hackers, the first real colonisers of cyberspace, believed that the Internet would

liberate us from gender . . . Why would it matter, in this brave new networked world, what sort of body you had? And if your body didn't matter, why would it matter if you were a man or a woman, a boy or a girl, or something else entirely?[47]

But Penny does now know that it does matter, and that it matters in new and occasionally frightening ways. As she says of her present experience rather than her past hopes:

> Like many women with any sort of profile online, I'm used to messages of this sort – the violent rape and torture fantasies, the threats to my family and personal safety, the graphic emails with my face crudely pasted on to pictures of pornographic models performing sphincter-stretchingly implausible feats of physical endurance.[48]

To be '*used to*' these forms of attack is to have to work in an everyday situation in which women are graphically abused and in which they rightly have very real concerns about their personal safety and that of friends and family. In the global world of the web, this kind of abuse has been the lot of both individual women and women in general. The very terms 'woman' and 'feminism' have come to attract internet trolls, the new, entirely unlovely inhabitants of cyberspace.

There are many, both conservative and libertarian, voices which suggest that this kind of abuse about women and feminism should not be taken too seriously; it is suggested that this abuse is 'just' fantasy and that it would be wrong to try and censor the free expression of views. To which it is only possible to retort that to threaten physical violence against another human being has long been taken as a criminal offence. To allow this threat to go unchallenged is to throw aside all the assumptions and values of any civilized society, namely that every human being has a right to live without threats of violence from any of their fellow citizens. Even to suggest that these threats are 'not serious' abandons all that work and all that resistance to arbitrary power which have been established over the centuries.

Rich fantasy lives may be what we all wish for, and what might fuel and inspire all kinds of creative engagement. But threats of murder and various forms of assault are not rich and potentially creative forms of fantasy; on the contrary, they are forms of fantasy which suggest hurt, loss and fear rather than the wish to debate with others. Many of those trolls writing the 'hate mail' to women (and to a lesser extent to gay people) would no doubt wish to think of themselves as powerful 'Masters of the Universe' (to refer to the title of the book about the champions of neoliberalism by Daniel Stedman Jones), living lives of sophisticated metropolitan privilege. To suggest that these people are threatened, in the same way as the 'forgotten' white, working-class, unskilled and materially underprivileged people who support UKIP in the present-day UK or idiot religious fundamentalism in the United States, would no doubt be regarded by them as slanderous. Yet both groups, the privileged and the poor, share a powerful sense of social and personal discontent: they are not living the lives which they assumed would be theirs. For supporters of UKIP, the threatening others are a general group called 'foreigners', with a supporting and also important sub-group called 'bureaucrats' or perhaps more colloquially 'the health and safety'. This latter group stands accused of stopping every form of initiative with senseless legislation and intervention. Despite the fact that it is, precisely, unskilled male workers who are most vulnerable to the flagrant absence of health-and-safety procedures, a fantastical connection is made between potential energy and its suppression by various legal and quasi-legal forms.

Many of the people writing abuse about Laurie Penny or others are not, however, in this same category of the poor and the unskilled, and would no doubt be appalled to be discussed on the same page. The threat to these writers is the very real one of their failure to be able to compete successfully in what has become the increasingly precarious and toxic world of employment in neoliberal economies. Very few individuals, throughout the world, are now employed in secure jobs, with clear benefits and reliable prospects. On the contrary, the world of work has been radically destabilized, and it is increasingly normal for work to be organized through short-term contracts and endless forms of assessment and appraisal. These new worlds build not communities of work but competitive contexts of employment, in which it is entirely consistent with those environments for individuals to be wary and suspicious of others. Much middle-class and professional work – indeed, any job with a hierarchical career structure – had interpersonal competition written into it in the past, but what has changed is the degree to which failing to succeed now comes with increasingly negative consequences. For anyone, work in these contexts is replete with anxiety.

But for men, white, middle-class, educated men, this new world of work offers much less of the security and a great deal more of the insecurity of the workplaces known to their fathers and indeed to a few of their mothers. Given that social mobility in both the UK and the USA has become, since the financial crisis that began in 2007, virtually stagnant, and the competition for access to privileged higher education increasingly frantic, the psychic burden of possible failure, of slipping off the ladder which allows the continuation of privilege, is considerable if not overwhelming.[49] When this frenzied world of workplace worry then allows into it women, and both men and women who are not white and who are not heterosexual, the psychic burden is elaborated and enlarged, not just through fantasies of what might happen to the job prospects of the traditionally secure, but because of how this might happen through the literal presence of those others who embody this fantasy of engulfment. To a young, white, middle-class man brought up within the highly ritualized expectations of the fusion of academic success with social success and financial reward, the different others who invade his space are a real threat, not least because these 'others' may well operate within quite different and unfamiliar sets of norms and values. Cyberspace allows a very open world for the expression of these fears.

So this new geography of the workplace becomes a site from which the threatened project their fears about the loss of security onto those who appear as hostile and disruptive. In this context and in this dynamic, new sites of contest are created for feminism and feminist politics. This is also an example of the way in which there is no time limit, no date of irrelevance, for feminism: as the organization of the worlds within which we live change, so the sites of gendered privilege change, as do – and should – both the focus of feminist politics and the complexities of gendered relations.

Here then, it is important to consider the ways in which feminism changes in terms of the issues presented by various forms of change, and why the differences between generations of feminism are often, and arguably mistakenly, discussed in terms of differences only in terms of feminism, and not in terms of the often considerable changes in the social world as a whole.

One of the many aspects of feminist history that can be gleaned from reading feminist accounts of the past, or feminist writing in the past, is that there is, rather than that disruption between generations that is often suggested, a very high degree of similarity and agreement. In this, it is of course necessary to separate what has changed in terms of wider social shifts: for example, a feminist writing in the nineteenth century could no more give the title *The Vagina Monologues* to a play for a public audience than Emily Bronte could allow, in *Wuthering Heights*, Heathcliff and the young Catherine Earnshaw a fully realized sexual relationship.[50] We have to be content, if we read Emily Bronte or any of the other great women writers of the nineteenth century, with flashes of lightning and other forces of nature as indications of sexual attraction. Fuller details of heterosexual intercourse in mainstream fiction had to wait – at least legitimately – until the second half of the twentieth century.

The impact of forms of censorship, and what we make of them, is just one example of the reason that we might approach with some caution the idea that there are distinct and often apparently unbridgeable differences between the experiences of different generations of feminists. One aspect of modernity that bridges generations is that of the hunger for sensation and sensational subjects, which impacts upon feminism quite as much as it does on other aspects of the twenty-first century. Thus the possible headline 'Young feminists blast older generation' is much more interesting than a headline which reads 'Young feminists agree that gender inequality continues'. That latter headline would be in the tradition of the journalist Claud Cockburn's famous fantasy headline, 'Small earthquake in Chile, not many dead': a matter of no significance and of little interest to readers or viewers. The global media of the twenty-first century is endlessly hungry for drama; when there are no extraordinary stories at hand, then they can be constructed out of moral panics. John Jervis in particular has written persuasively about the appetite of modernity for sensation: 'Since the eighteenth century, Western modernity has been deeply embedded in a body-focused culture of spectacle and sensation . . . being present from very early on in the way we both conceive of, and experience, our relations with each other and the wider world.'[51] Much of sensationalism and moral panic emerges from the politics of the right (for example, the stories about immigrants taking 'our' jobs or the presence of al-Qaeda on every street corner), but feminism has not been entirely exempt from the same dramatizing energy. In accounts of the disappearance and/or the rebirth of feminism, we can see at work that subtle, but distorting, pressure to organize social reality in favour of some form of extraordinary spectacle. Books with titles such as *The End of Men* or *Is the Future Female?* all implicitly dramatize aspects of social change.[52]

So central to any feminist engagement with the world of the twenty-first century has to be a recognition of the ways in which politics – of all shapes and forms – is, and to a certain extent has been since the eighteenth century, constructed through the expectations of change and sensation, *both of which obscure continuity.* If we return to the very beginnings of self-consciously feminist writing in the seventeenth century in the global north – the work of both Mary Astell and the anonymous author of 'Woman Not Inferior to Man' – we find the arguments about gender and gender inequality presented in terms of an immediate problem, a question that demands urgent answer. Here is literary and journalistic sensationalism in its earliest days; centuries later Beauvoir would write of *The Second Sex*, Germaine Greer of *The Female Eunuch*, Susan Faludi of *Backlash*, all titles that suggest not the persistent, endlessly reproduced quality of everyday forms of gendered inequality and the lives lived through it, but revelations of individual and social relations.

It is admittedly very difficult for any radical political project to infuse its potential members with enthusiasm if what is presented to them is a picture of the complexities of the lives of most people, in which the bad and the good, the unbearable and the bearable, are often intertwined. This has become much more difficult in the global north in the twentieth and twenty-first century, given that some aspects of the glaring poverty of the nineteenth and first half of the twentieth century have disappeared, as have many legal distinctions between men and women. The material and the institutional worlds have shifted towards the expectation, if not the practice, of greater gender equality; pious hopes about its furtherance are generally expressed and shared. But at the same time, and notwithstanding the continued national and international energy and resources given to enlarging forms of gender equality, there are two other social processes which minimize the achievement of gender equality. The first is the now well-documented increase in social inequality, particularly in the UK and the United States. In many ways, this is *the* sensational story of the second decade of the twenty-first century. It is not, however, a story which has not been told, and there are now many brilliant and persuasive accounts of this phenomenon. But in very few of those accounts (those by Chang, Dorling, Jones, Piketty) does the *specific* situation of women emerge. The paradox of the documentation of what is an appalling enlargement of social inequality which ignores the specificity of inequalities of either gender or race is, variously, unfortunate, depressing or quite simply short-sighted. For feminism, this intellectual exclusion should not be unfamiliar, but the question remains of how to address the issue without adopting either a political or analytical position which simply adds women to an existing narrative, or constructs the various forms of discrimination against women as a separate issue, unconnected to that of general forms of social inequality.

The importance of not doing this, and instead of writing a feminist narrative which unites work on social inequality with the recognition of gender inequality is now urgent: there are far too many people, throughout the world, women and men, who live together in conditions of appalling poverty for us to allow accounts of inequality to be located within a vision blind to both the ties and the abuses of gender. Further, the part that the existence and the continuity of gender difference and gender inequality plays in social inequality should not be confined to discussions about the possible social implications of the theoretical disappearance of the gendered human subject. Without returning to debates between Nancy Fraser and Judith Butler, it is crucially important to recognize that capitalism has shown itself to be a system of some adaptive competence, more than able to entertain (and absorb) changes in expectations about gender. Nevertheless, all the evidence – about material rewards and institutional power – suggests that masculinity is more widely rewarded and deemed more appropriate to the exercise of power than femininity is. In 1997, Linda McDowell wrote of the ways in which, in the professional culture of the City of London, the expression of the feminine in men was often welcomed, but that of masculine traits by women was not. In 2014, Kristen Schilt and Lauren wrote of the way in which women who had transitioned to men found their job prospects markedly improved.[53]

All feminists would – almost by definition – have to agree that the 'death' of men, in terms of their greater presence in positions of power, is much exaggerated. What many, if not all, feminists would also point out is that the alliances between women and men who regard any further shift in the allocation of power and material reward for women and men as being socially problematic is as powerful in the twenty-first century as it was in the nineteenth and twentieth. Those simplistic 'progress' narratives of changes in the social position of women inevitably deny two aspects of those changes. The first is that those changes occurred rather less through social pressures and/or political campaigning than is sometimes supposed, and rather more because of other events and other social needs. The second is the persistence, across place and time, of forms of alliances (across races and genders) that resist any alteration in the status quo of gender. For example, women and men united in Britain to resist the extension of the suffrage to women, just as very similar alliances argued, and argue, that equal pay for equal work or the further extension of welfare rights such as maternity and paternity pay would bankrupt the country.[54] Any reading of the past two hundred years of the history of either Britain or the United States would very rapidly come across the persistent belief in some quarters that these vastly rich countries cannot provide either welfare benefits or extended access to power. This view – which has assumed a new legitimacy and force in the context of neoliberal economics and politics – would wish populations to believe that wealthy countries of the global west are balanced on

some precarious knife edge of social and economic survival, which
any further demands from any section of the population would
seriously imperil.

This view, in which it is all too easy for politicians to revive
slogans that may well have had some purchase at times of real
national danger ('we are all in this together' being the most
recently brought back to life), add drama and a sense of insecurity to everyday existence. Much time and ink, both feminist and
otherwise, has been devoted to considering the reasons for the
vitriolic hatred expressed by male trolls writing on the internet
about women, and many of those accounts have turned to psychoanalytical explanations, based in part on theoretical assumptions
about our human capacity for both love and hate of our mothers.
These sources of emotional energy are present in us all, and it is
perhaps at least as useful, rather than turning to trans-historical
explorations of the general human psyche, to turn to the social
values and ideas to which citizens are exposed in the early twenty-
first century. Amongst these is that of the precarious, fragile nature
of our social world and the need to maintain an absolute control
over any person, people or ideas which might threaten it. Thus
it is not just that for many people across the world, everyday life
itself has become more precarious – which it certainly always was
and equally certainly is becoming – but that we are encouraged to
believe in the pointlessness, even in some cases the socially unacceptable form, of any changes other than those which reinforce the
normative order of neoliberalism. To challenge this – as women
and men might wish to do through their understanding of the
values and politics of feminism – is to be seen to be proposing an
attack on a way of life and a set of values that have been at the core
of an individual's existence.

Social anxiety may thus be at least as important a part of
understanding that internet hatred of which Penny and others
have written as are explanations about the working of the human
psyche. But there is one further aspect of contemporary feminism
that needs to be repeated here: the way in which some feminist
narratives can themselves exhibit that inclination towards the
dramatic that is an inevitable part of the culture of modernity. To
say, for example, that women have never been so vulnerable to

domestic violence as they currently are in Britain or the United States is more dramatic, and more potentially viable as a headline, than arguments suggesting that the roots of violence in personal relationships have complex and long-standing origins. The former may or may not be true (the question of the extent of violence in the past is unknowable), but it prevents us from examining, for instance, the many ways in which the global north has come to increase the contexts in which individuals have to compete with one another, and the social consequences of that extended competition. The fierce, almost feral, violence with which some parents now compete for the educational places that will guarantee the social reproduction of privilege is just one instance of the culture that we are encouraged to endorse. Amy Chua's *Battle Hymn of the Tiger Mother*, an account of the educational 'grooming' of her children, was met with critical but also many supportive voices, voices which suggested that 'these' days there was 'no choice' except that of intense academic socialization from birth.[55]

In this that ancient idea of 'doing your best for your child' has come to be increasingly focused on educational performance, and through it the hoped-for access to the replication of social wealth and power. At the same time, we have to recognize that those very institutions – schools and universities – that could be providing an understanding of education as something other than a preparation for the labour market are increasingly colluding – and such is the case across the globe – with an entirely instrumental view of their function. For example, the increasingly frequent convention by which first-year students at university are being addressed on the matter of how to use the format of academic work as a way of providing material for their CVs is part of that process. The results of this view of education are visible in the BBC television programme *The Apprentice*, now seen on both sides of the Atlantic. Endless young people mouth inanities about their entrepreneurial zeal and competence, only to be summarily dismissed because they have proved themselves to be incapable of thought, critical judgement or what is described on the programme as 'common sense'. The richly ironic confrontation in which a committed spokesperson for entrepreneurial values repeatedly dismisses young people who have no 'sense' outside the confines of entrepreneurial rhetoric is a poignant reflection on the causes of the inability of the youthful zombies to think.

Thus the paradox emerges in which the expressed values of higher education in a neoliberal world come to exhibit precisely those characteristics which make it so unfit for the purpose of the continued understanding of that world – or indeed of any other – and so fertile a breeding ground for greed and the thoughtless pursuit of profit. Neither of these is new to human societies, but the integration of these values into various forms of social infra-structure is to the detriment not just of various institutions but of social relations, and in this context, relations between women and men. Scarcity and insecurity bring enmity between individuals and countries, furthered by education systems which are justified in terms of their ability to 'help us to compete in global markets'. That quotation comes from no specific source, but it could come from almost any university prospectus about the 'value' of education, or from any neoliberal politician responsible for the reproduction of social human capital. Yet recognition of the drawbacks and inher-ent difficulties of these ideas comes less from politicians than from often surprising sources. For example, Mark Carney, the governor of the Bank of England, was quoted in 2014 as saying 'unchecked market fundamentalism can devour the social capital essential for the long-term dynamism of capitalism itself.'[56] When a gover-nor of the Bank of England explicitly recognizes the sociologist Pierre Bourdieu's ideas about the importance of 'social capital', it is apparent that there are considerable fissures in governing elites; the question remains as to whether or not political parties across the political and global spectrum can even begin to understand the impact of the erosion of social capital on the stability of capitalism.

For many feminists, concerned (rightly) with issues such as violence against women and the internet abuse of women, these questions about the social consequences of the implementation of policies of unbridled 'market fundamentalism' may seem to be a long way from the politics of feminism. But here the argument is that these questions are entirely and absolutely fundamental to feminism; fundamental because of the ways in which individuals, and individual women and men, are increasingly pitted against one another in what might be seen, in the more nightmarish scenarios of life in the twenty-first century, as a feeding frenzy for those paltry remaining rewards of capitalism which have not been devoured by the very rich. In this frantic competition it is more than likely that those most disadvantaged by the new conditions of life will be two groups: those who take the responsibility for the care of others, and those for whom social mores restrict their access to the crucial skills that provide material reward. As readers will recognize, these groups are largely made up of women. In the concluding pages of this chapter, what are proposed are three arguments with which feminism has to engage in order to halt what is potentially not just the continuation of gender inequality, but its worsening.

First, it is essential – as it is for anyone concerned with social justice – that we recognize that we do not live in a world created by 'natural' events but in a world born out of human agency and choice. That this agency and these choices have brought us to a point where governments (certainly not all, but many across the globe) subscribe to political agendas which demonize and impoverish the most vulnerable has to be a starting point. To engage with the world through any of those comforting lenses called 'progress' or 'change' or 'development' is deliberately to choose a degree of social short-sightedness, a wilful denial of the structural changes that are taking place (for example, attacks on all forms of state support) in favour of reference to marginal 'improvements' (for example, in terms of the greater representation of women in elite positions). In terms of this latter example, what is also suggested here is the possibility that the mantra that 'power corrupts' might actually apply to women as much as men. Certainly the mantra need not apply to everyone, but that very possibility also allows that it might apply to some.

The second point that needs careful thought and attention is that of the implications of any political campaign that protests against the degradation of women. This is not to argue against any of the campaigns that protest, for example, against the objectification of women in the media, in fashion or online. This is a form of abuse, and should be seen as such: real and damaging abuse of human individuals that should invoke legal redress for the harm that it does. But the point is that the redress should be legal (and therefore carry the chances of punishment) rather than moral. Outrage (such as that about pornographic representations of women and children) all too often leads to moralistic campaigns. Those moral campaigns, initiated by sections of the press, are as much about its own profitability as about any meaningful intervention against those constructing the material. If the gross national product of the United Kingdom now includes the income from pornography and prostitution, it would seem only reasonable to assume that these activities – clearly seen as perfectly *legal* – should also be subject to what would appear to be, in this case, the rather short arm of the law.

The third and final point concerns the discussion of gender inequality in terms of those psychic dynamics of all human beings of which psychoanalysis has made us aware. There are now increasing numbers of people who understand and appreciate the value of psychoanalytic theory, and the value of its possibilities as a 'talking cure' for those afflicted by various forms of emotional distress. One of those forms of distress has been – and remains – the insecurity which people have had about their gender identity. This insecurity has been, as every history of sexuality tells us, sometimes punished with various degrees of cruelty by individuals and institutions. The entirely liberating and welcome view that for all of us our gender identity is insecure and ambiguous is one for which we have to thank psychoanalysis. But from this, and through psychoanalysis, it is arguably dangerous to build feminist campaigns that do not consider the difference between theories about the individual human psyche and theories about society. It is also the case that this link has long intrigued and preoccupied many writers (not least Freud himself), and to assume that feminist readings of psychoanalytic theory have now uncovered that long-sought holy grail of the links between the individual and the general is perhaps premature. Various members of the Frankfurt School – over fifty years ago – pointed out the possible connections between the authority structures of the German family and the acceptance of German fascism, but as they also pointed out, this connection was made through the coming into existence of a social theory that had at its core a recognition of the impact on human beings of material as well as psychic factors.

We therefore need to proceed with great care if we are to argue that from the existing patterns of our psychic world or the rewritten possibilities of the gender order we can explain or rebut an existing social order, or build a new one. This kind of causal assumption removes far too much from what makes us all human, social, actors, not least among those factors our social ambitions, aspirations, individual needs and circumstances. Crucially, we are all porous: we learn and we are influenced by ideas outside our families and our immediate circumstances, and inevitably some of those acquired beliefs are more acceptable to some than to others. We do not all — and that all includes women as much as men — acquire values sympathetic to feminism. The uncomfortable conclusion that we might draw from that is that rather than attempting to make feminism a broad church, we might consider making it a rather more defined church, one that moves away from the fundamentalism inherent in essentialism and towards a more defined, and socially coherent, vision of the meaning and origin of gendered inequality.

5

Making Gender Equality

Let other pens, as the great Jane Austen wrote of the fate of two of her characters in her novel *Mansfield Park*, dwell on guilt and misery. Writing about the question of gender inequality in the twenty-first century could encourage that same reaction, given its seemingly endless reproduction. Despite the various changes for the better that have taken place, and are taking place, throughout the world in the lives of many people, there are also far too many instances where new forms of inequality, both general and specifically gendered, are emerging. Indeed, Austen's comment suggests to us something of the resignation that can sometimes be encountered in discussions about gender inequality, that 'life is just like that', or that it will always be the case that the fortunes of men are destined by nature to be different from – and often superior to – those of women. If we wish to set aside this passive acceptance, we have to look clearly at the problematic issue of what has changed in the situation of women in the past two hundred years, but also of what has not changed.

In the global north, and increasingly in much of the global south, two recognizable shifts have occurred since the mid-1960s which have had a major impact on relations between women and men: the availability of effective contraception and the increasing erosion of what was once the legal principle of 'coverture'. The wish to separate heterosexual intercourse from the conception of children is as ancient as human history, but it is only very recently that this has become generally possible and acceptable. The history of 'coverture', the principle of English law through which it was established that married women should be subject to the control of their husbands, is that it has been gradually abandoned since the eighteenth century.[1] Similar changes are now becoming things of the past, at least in legal terms, in much of the west. But two points are very important here, the first of which is the often long time lag between the identification of practices which affect the physical well-being of women and effective action against them.

To take just two examples to illustrate this, both in the context of the British political system: the issue of female genital mutilation was first raised in the House of Commons by the Duchess of Atholl in 1929, yet it was not until 1985 that the first Act of Parliament (the Prohibition of Female Circumcision Act) was successfully introduced, by the Conservative MP Marion Roe. There is no reliable date for the first discussion of domestic violence against women (a violence which continues to kill four women a week in their homes in the UK), but it was only in 1976 that the Domestic Violence and Matrimonial Proceedings Act finally became statute, through the efforts of the Labour MP Jo Richardson.

The second point is the persistence of the ancient and very important concept of authority, and especially symbolic authority, being invested in men rather than women. For example, it was not until 2014 that the Church of England accepted the idea that women could become bishops, and other churches and other religions still maintain an absolute refusal of the idea that women can legitimately represent any form of religious authority. The literature on women and symbolic authority suggests that it is extremely difficult to challenge the association of that particular form of authority with men; reformers have been consistently thwarted by arguments about 'separate but equal', the 'authority of the text' and the 'natural' roles of women and men. All these assertions have had their equivalent in arguments about both racial and classed inequality; 'natural' explanations of human difference that have increasingly been rejected, although still capable of reappearing endlessly in all parts of the world.

From the various tirades that have often been voiced against equality (be it of race, class or gender), we might assume that human beings are 'naturally' meant to compete with one another. Jacqueline Rose, in 2014, posed the question of whether or not there is something about sexual difference that produces violence.[2] The idea of 'the war of all against all' is a familiar part of western political philosophy, one recognized quite as much as the equally ancient belief in human equality. From the days of 'When Adam delved and Eve span, who was then the gentleman?', to the opening sentences of the constitution of the United States, to proclamations in the twentieth century from the United Nations about human rights, there are powerful traditions which assert the fundamental equality of all human beings. The meaning of the word 'men', those who were, according to the US constitution of 1776, all 'created equal', has gradually been refined to include women and non-white people in much of the world; but what has not changed – and here we meet the very foundations of the making of gendered inequality – is the construction of 'equality' in terms of the rights that have been presumed to be initially and primarily those of men.

The Rights of Women

This leaves, and has always left, those who wish to see gender equality achieved in the position of doing two things. One is playing 'catch up' with men, in the sense that what women demand are various forms of access to the same kind of treatment and inclusion as those given to men. Traditionally, these rights have included the right to the autonomy and control of the self, to vote, to be educated and to enter the professions and the public world. A second, more radical possibility is that of thinking about the achievement of gender equality less in terms of this coincidence with male experience and more in terms that relate specifically to the situations and the lives encountered by the majority of women:

lives of care giving and of the need, throughout the world, to combine the responsibilities of care with paid work. This does not mean that *only* the lives of women would be transformed, but the ways in which we think about our model of the 'person' would incorporate a different – and arguably much wider – understanding of human responsibilities and possibilities. The first approach to equality involves changes in statute, be it the statutes of a country or those of a particular institution. The complexity of change that is involved here is often both fundamental and yet at the same time limited; significant as it was, the 1928 Act of Parliament in the UK that gave the vote to all men and all women over 21, regardless of property qualifications, involved little reorganization of the social world. The symbolic importance may have been considerable but the social restructuring involved was minimal.

Against this, we have to set the kind of rethinking of the social world and its many and varied arrangements which might be involved in making the playing field of life level for both women and men. The difficulties of this are such as to challenge the most determined supporter of gender equality, and it is today apparent that many of the previously favoured options for producing this state have proved to have little impact, or only impact on those who already have some degree of social privilege. The most favoured means of ensuring greater gender equality has always been education. To refuse education for girls is now regarded as the most absurd and outrageous infringement of individual liberty, and access to education is regarded as the norm for much of the world. But as many generations of girls and young women have found, the worlds outside the classroom and the university are not always receptive to the goal of gender equality, and whilst the assumption of education for girls is now (almost) the global norm, the worlds encountered after education may radically limit gender equality. Very few countries, then as now, have done much to ensure that the world after education accords women the same material rewards as those of men. There are, throughout the world, numerous studies which demonstrate that whilst equal numbers of women and men enter, for example, medical training, ten years after graduation the numbers of women still actively engaged in that profession are paid less and are less likely to be promoted than men. This is, admittedly, an example drawn from a highly regarded, and generally well-paid, profession, but the same pattern persists across all forms of paid work: entry (with a few notable exceptions, such as training for the Roman Catholic priesthood) is open to women and men, but reward and access to power, however limited both may be, are consistently greater for men than for women. And we should always remember – a fact of social life too often forgotten by liberal feminism – that it is not just that the rewards of paid work are fewer for women than men, but that the rewards of paid work for at least a third of the population, both male and female, in both Britain and the United States, are barely sufficient for subsistence.

In what has been said here, it is hoped that a vein of scepticism about well-meaning schemes for 'opening up' various forms of employment to women is detected. This is not a critique of these schemes per se, but it is a resistance to those almost magical powers that are sometimes invested in education. There is no case against education in itself and for itself, but there has to be a discussion about what we think we are going to change when we invoke the traditional paths to gender equality, of which education is the most often named. One of the most potent arguments about the impact of education on any population as a whole is that it enhances and reproduces social inequality; even the most optimistic enthusiast for the radical possibilities of education must recognize the ways in which the existing (largely family-based) social and cultural capital of an individual provides enhanced opportunities for educational success. Given that elite educational establishments across the world are remarkably similar in their resistance to forms of what they identify as 'social engineering' ,and have unshakeable confidence in their ability to detect in 18-year-olds what they define as 'academic promise', it is not surprising that what occurs in those contexts is a consistent form of social reproduction.[3]

For small numbers of women, however, the opening up of the professions and higher education has provided access to worlds traditionally dominated by men. As of now, there is no evidence that the arrival of individual women in these worlds has produced significant change; institutional culture has shown itself to be very resilient to ideas about gender and racial equality. Thus the changes hoped for by both the suffrage movement and campaigns for the education of women have proved to be far more limited in practice: the past hundred years have suggested that legislative change about the incorporation of women into institutional politics does not automatically achieve greater gender equality. Some women (more or less exclusively members of the Labour Party) spoke in the British House of Commons in the twentieth century in favour of measures such as family allowances and equal pay, but others did not.[4] If it is not the law that brings about change in the relations between institutions and women, and between men and women as individuals, we then have to ask how change has occurred and how it might be extended. (Here the exception to the limited impact of education is that of those countries or cultures where education is actually forbidden to women, either by law itself or by custom. No such historical pattern existed in much of the world: for centuries, the pattern was much more usually that very few people had any education at all, but education itself was not specifically forbidden to women.)

One of the conventional views of historians and social scientists about what is fancifully called the 'emancipation' of women is that it was achieved by social change: new technologies and new forms of production bringing with them new needs and new social expectations. For example, the industrialization of Britain, which initially provided some employment for women (although throughout the nineteenth century, the primary form of employment for unmarried women was that of a servant in a private home), subsequently needed a literate workforce to service a developing infrastructure. That infrastructure included shops and offices, places where unmarried women were – and are – employed in significant numbers. Subsequent developments of welfare services (including education) in their turn demanded teachers and nurses, again consistent forms of women's employment.[5] Wars, essentially the two world wars, are often credited with speeding up the acceptance of women into various forms of employment, but two aspects of this assertion should be remembered: that, contrary to popular views, many women were in paid employment before these wars, and that powerful ideologies resisted (and this was most notable in Nazi Germany) the paid employment of women and often specifically of married women. Both Britain and the United States made much of campaigns about the valuable war work of women, but the importance of this work was often as much about the propaganda merits of 'we're all in this together' as any lasting extension of women's access to previously male employment. No women, we might recall, ever appear, or even existed, as the individuals who directed either of the world wars, and it remains possible to watch almost any western film or television version of the Second World War without seeing a single woman occupying any position of authority. If women do appear, it is, for example, as the sorrowing mother in the film *Saving Private Ryan*. The part of women in that pivotal war – the war that remains central to the west's views of its moral legitimacy – is largely unrecorded.

In considering the reality of that famous advertisement slogan for cigarettes, 'You've come a long way, baby', Gramsci's comment about himself, 'I'm a pessimist because of intelligence, but an optimist because of will', seems entirely apt, since it provides us with a terse reminder of the need to assess convenient social myths with a very considerable degree of scepticism.[6] Indeed, quite as much as Gramsci's epigrammatic comment, a great deal of what was written elsewhere in Europe by political and intellectual radicals of the 1920s and the 1930s (for example, the work of the Frankfurt School and that of Georg Simmel) can seem as relevant to contemporary politics as it was in its time, often surpassing more recent, highly specialized, studies of the social worlds in its ambition to make connections between the 'inner self' and material and economic circumstances. In at least some more recent work, what is obscured is the long-term continuation, throughout the global north and the global south, of consistent patterns of social inequality, of which the inequalities resultant from gender difference are a major aspect. It sometimes appears as if social commentators (be they academics or otherwise) have actually believed that slogan about women coming 'a long way'. In the face of this view, in which surface changes of dress and bodily stance become invested with an importance that is otherwise generally denied to fashion, it is necessary to propose another view: that gender inequality has not disappeared, but its forms have changed.

If we look at the various ways in which the lives of contemporary women differ from those of our grandmothers, we
immediately recognize that much of women's work occupies a
different social and spatial space from that of our predecessors.
Very few women, in the global north, now toil in the same way as
fifty or a hundred years ago: the mechanization of the home, and
contraception, have decreased the sheer physical labour involved
in the maintenance of a household. But against this we have to set
the numbers of other hours which women work outside the home:
the majority of women with children are now in part-time work,
whilst virtually all women without children are in full-time work.
In these sentences, what is apparent is the way in which the distinction of having and not having children impacts to a greater extent
on women than on men. The employment patterns of very few
men are affected by whether or not they have children: however
important the birth of children might be to men in other ways, it
has a virtually negligible effect on their participation in paid work.
The stability of this pattern, with accompanying effects – such as
that of progress within a career structure for those mothers in jobs
which have such a thing – demonstrates the long-term continuity of the association of women with care. But aside from these
important ways in which the intersections of care, domestic life
and paid work can act to the disadvantage of women, there are
too the increasingly demanding narratives about the home and
domestic life. In the first chapter the idea of the 'ideal home' and its
perfect occupants was mentioned in the context of the discussion
of the various housing crises of the west. These crises obviously
impinge radically, and negatively, on the lives of both women and
men, but women are arguably more subject to those expectations
raised, in brief, by the title of Nigella Lawson's cookery book, *How
To Be a Domestic Goddess*.[7] The title is a highly conscious parody of
ideas about happy housewives, but at the same time it is a demanding idea, an idea that speaks to created and profitable ideas about
how to nurture. The cultural historian Raphael Samuel, writing
about what he has called 'retrochic', notes the explosion of advertising terms which 'make a feature of being "pure", "fresh" and
"natural"'.[8] What can be seen in both these instances is a forceful
narrative which assures women that, as their lives become ever

more complex and demanding, they still remain within that apparently blissful space of makers of hearth and home.

So the question arises of why and how we consistently turn to fantasies of a more 'natural' past. This is especially pertinent at the point where material circumstances are rapidly putting into question one of the pivotal explanations for women's under-representation in the public world: that women 'naturally' want to spend time caring for their children and others. This endlessly reiterated argument has always homogenized women, whilst at the same time avoiding difficult questions about those women whose circumstances do not allow them this choice: circumstances in which freedom of choice, the exercise of that 'natural' capacity to care, becomes available only to those with the material wealth to enable it. Yet as economic pressures on all households increase, and as the idea of citizenship is increasingly framed within normative definitions of the employed and currently famous 'hard-working' subject, so ideas about 'good' women have been changing. No longer is it the case that sexual purity and the keeping of the domestic flame remain central to definitions of acceptable femininity. The 'shame' of women, which, as Clara Fischer has pointed out, was once produced through sexual 'misbehaviour', is now more likely to be produced through what Emma Casey and Imogen Tyler have located as the 'shame' of the inability to provide for their children.[9] The demonization of the so-called 'welfare mothers' is both reframing the location of the 'shame' of women in absence from the workforce, and at the same time informing aspirational fantasies about what 'naturally' good mothers want for their children. Whilst women remain the subject of ancient expectations about natural 'caring' and 'nurturing' abilities, so those very assumptions provide justifications for the minimal rewards often given to those who perform those 'natural' tasks in the paid work which is becoming essential for every adult, whatever their other responsibilities.

What also has to be said here is that most governments throughout the world fail to provide effective or adequate support for all forms of the work of care. The usual argument against the state provision of child care (or state care for others who might require it) is that it is not the state's responsibility to do this. As neoliberal economics tighten their stranglehold on the world's governments, it is likely that the extent of the state provision of all forms of care will go down rather than up. Where adequate provision is made, which is in a very few countries, evidence does suggest that the impact on gender equality is not as substantial as might be supposed.[10] These aspects of the general discussion of the relationship between gendered responsibility for all forms of care and the production of gendered inequality suggests that there are two predominant – and global – narratives about possible changes: one is that the state should provide meaningful care for children and others as a means to the further 'emancipation' of women, and the other is that mothers should be able to 'choose' the extent to which they are in paid work. In both cases, the narratives need urgent deconstruction. In the first, it has to be made clear that paid work is not necessarily the absorbing and well paid work that is the general expectation and assumption of many privileged groups, but rather a fundamental and compelling necessity for economic survival. 'Emancipation' has very little to do with hours spent stacking supermarket shelves or working in a call centre. This is about the provision of the means of existence. The second narrative, that mothers in particular should be able to 'choose' whether or not they are in paid work, ignores, as much as the discourse about 'emancipation', the different economic circumstances of mothers. 'Choice' in a market economy, and one increasingly dominated by neoliberal economics, is not available to everyone.

Arguments about the state provision of child care and its impact on women are, however, something of a luxury for most women on the planet. Many countries, notably the 'old' Soviet empire, have abolished rather than increased many of the supportive frameworks which assumed that all adults, male and female, would be in work throughout their lives. It is only in a minority of countries, we have to remember, that the mere idea of state-supported child care has been considered, let alone introduced. Most notably, the world's most powerful country, the United States, has absolutely no universal, state-provided child-care provision, let alone legislation allowing maternity and paternity leave. That country, and its adoring satellites, might well remember that its record on the structures that might support the 'emancipation' of women, so often a feature of rhetorical justifications for its foreign policy, is abysmal. For women, indeed all parents, in countries such as the United States in the global north, and many of the countries in the global south, child care is a matter for the individual parent to arrange. This ensures with absolute certainty that material inequality will come to dominate these arrangements. Those with well-paid jobs will be able to 'choose' excellent child care; those without will have to put together a patchwork of reliance on relatives and poorly paid minders.

The general provision of state care, be it for children or others, was long a feature of many socialist societies and of those – such as Israel – with a very clear political agenda about the making of future citizens. State socialism has now disappeared from most of the world, and what is left in its place, as far as agendas about the ending of gender inequality are concerned, is a world in which national politics (and national politics about welfare arrangements) are increasingly at the mercy – or more particularly, the lack of mercy – of powerful global corporations. Politics that are framed in terms of the necessary conditions for these institutions to flourish are defined in terms of needs for a workforce skilled in ways appropriate to the interests of the company, the lack of regulation and low rates of corporate taxation. What they do not speak of is the responsibility of employers to provide welfare benefits for their employees, or to pay the rate of tax that might make these provisions possible. Whilst these employers might be increasingly gender blind in the appointments that they make, at least at an entry or junior level, it is a form of blindness that rather readily disappears when faced with questions that affect their employees as parents or carers. The assumption that all citizens are 'care free' is one that operates to the very specific detriment of women.

The Limits of Liberalism

In the preceding section, it should have become clear that what is being argued is that any form of politics which wishes to engage with long-term, consistent, gender inequality has to engage with social inequality. It is simply not enough to suppose that the various forms of inequality that are the lot of women, across the wide spectrum of low pay, minimal presence in corporate boardrooms or absolute absence in many religious, military or legal hierarchies, can be addressed by multiple forms of different schemes. Historically and in contemporary terms, these schemes have addressed only particular sites of inequality, rather than the structural inequality that allows and has always allowed a minority of women to enjoy social privilege and power. From this we have to recognize that women, like men, are born into communities of class and race, both with their distinct cultures and their distinct forms of identity. If these communities are materially poor and closed in their views about education and the role of women, then it is – as numerous works of biography and autobiography have shown – extraordinarily difficult for individuals to leave those places which constitute both complex forms of supportive homes and encircling prisons.[11] In the eighteenth century, in the early days of the British market economy, the fictional character Moll Flanders may have been, as her author said, 'twelve years a Whore, five times a Wife (whereof once to her own brother), twelve years a Thief, eight years a transported Felon', but in the twenty-first century any one of these identities is likely to have a lasting impact on an individual.[12] We no longer live in that fluid world which Defoe imagined might emerge from the decline of royal power and the loss of religious authority. Without entirely endorsing the view of Max Weber that the 'iron' law of bureaucracy controls us all, we have to acknowledge that we are formed by our circumstances, and those circumstances include the ways in which we make our gender identity. Although various industries may have produced an often baffling array of consumer choice, these forms of choice are seldom real, and even less often reflected in other choices available to individuals.

In this, we have to recognize that the forms we choose for our gender identity are now less at the command of local circumstances than of influences largely removed from local circumstances. Almost nobody in the global north now lives in a village or a small town where behaviour is controlled and policed by neighbours and relatives. Instead we live in cities, and increasingly those mega cities of the twenty-first century where the ideas and the values which inform us come from distant origins. To sum up the juxtaposition of the various worlds of the twenty-first century, imagine a barefoot young person in a shanty town carrying a mobile phone and wearing a T-shirt that celebrates Madonna or David Beckham. Global brands, and with them global values, may still be intersected by those of specific communities, but they are nevertheless more present than in previous epochs, and are an important part of the world through which gender identity is acquired. For women, that gender identity is fundamentally about the body, its size, its appearance and its social fulfilment through economically independent existence. This human personification can be seen by anyone who has access to the internet. In this, the female body and person have become an essential part of the dynamic of consumption which drives and energizes capitalism. The labour of human beings was always the means by which economic systems maintained and reproduced themselves. But as technology reduced some of the need for specific forms of human labour, it was replaced by the repositioning of the body and particularly the female body as the locus of the dreams, desires and fantasies which make the re-creation and the profitable articulation of human needs possible. The exploitation to which this gives rise has already been mentioned, but a wider recognition is also necessary: that the existence of gender difference and the continued articulation of that condition which we call 'femininity' are an important part of capitalism's longevity. At the same time as feminism, and feminist fiction, have suggested the coming of androgyny and the merits of gender neutrality, evidence suggests that the creative possibilities of gender difference are equally energetically pursued, because of the contribution that their manufacture (both as fantasy and as reality) can make to that goal of 'growth' in global economies. This goal is not without its critics but it has, at the present time, a secure place in the lexicon of political rhetoric.[13]

That political rhetoric of growth seldom includes a discussion of the ways in which women, and femininity, might contribute to the greater productivity (and hence profit) of the world's economies, but it is impossible to contemplate 'growth' as it is now envisaged as taking place without the ongoing inclusion of women as both consumers and sites for the creation of fantasy. Women's ability to consume has been interrupted in recent years by the decline in the amount of disposable income available to much of the population, giving rise to those endlessly expressed fears about the economic health of 'the high street', a largely female location for spending. As basic costs of living rise, it is more than likely that more women – specifically women with dependent children – will be drawn into increasingly extended periods in the labour market, less as a result of emancipatory discourses or enhanced state arrangements for child care than through those same economic imperatives which have always drawn people, male and female, into paid work. Whilst some (amongst others, both some feminists and Marxists) might see this as a precondition or even a condition of women's greater equality and emancipation, more cautious observers might see this shift as nothing but the increasing insecurity of material existence.

This perception of the future – a central part of the imagination of George Orwell's dystopian novel *1984* – rests on the picture of the millions of the materially insecure who are working for a small and privileged elite. Yet in *1984*, the articulation and the demonstration of sexual difference have been outlawed. Everyone wears the same drab clothes, lives in the same identical buildings and eats the same appalling food. This vision does not consider the ways in which part of the longevity and the continued existence of capitalism depends upon the sale of goods, and many of those goods and services are related to the articulation and continuation of gender differences. Whilst Orwell certainly defined those authoritarian aspects of the state which are a perfectly possible aspect of the twenty-first century, what he failed to recognize were other forms of that state: a neoliberal, capitalist state explicitly committed to the private control of property. As the case of present-day China illustrates, the authoritarian state does not necessarily work to eradicate gender difference. Indeed, as Lisa Rofel has pointed out, China has been taught to 'desire' the goods that constitute the aspirational world of the west.[14]

Many people in the twenty-first century live, throughout the world, in contexts that are becoming, or remaining, in subtle and not so subtle ways, restrictive of various forms of individual behaviour. But one aspect of behaviour which is not restricted, is indeed encouraged, is the recognition and the continued and endless demonstration of gender differences: through fashion, through the sale of related services, from cosmetic surgery to hairdressing to 'romantic' tourism – all contexts in which gender and gender relations are crucial. Whether the sexual relations are those of the explicitly straight, transgender or gay worlds, what is being offered – and accepted – is the many varied ways in which gender identity can be adopted, discarded and re-created. A part of the shifting sands of gender identity remains that of the norm of the 'attractive', a norm which has been written and rewritten for centuries, but is now articulated in extensive elaborations of consumer possibilities.

Yet the social 'reach' of ideas and fantasies about appearance go very much further than mere interventions in the ageless questions of 'what to wear' or what constitutes human desirability. Part of what is so destructive about regimes around appearance is the anxiety produced about the fantasy of the ideal body. The picture of this body has been all too easy to produce and to distribute, given the range of globalized and highly commercialized versions of what women should look like. The psycho-sexual implications of body anxiety in women have achieved attention through evidence about the rising rates of eating disorders in young women, the cases of suicide in adolescent girls produced in part through concern about their bodies, and the persistent difficulties around questions of a personal aesthetic for women in public life. In all these cases, various voices have spoken against both the social pressures on women and the magnification of these pressures by sections of the media. But the more fundamental question, of the way in which gendered body anxiety is both a structurally supportive part of twenty-first-century material relations and a contributory factor in the persistence of gender inequality, is seldom addressed. These anxieties around the body, increasingly a part of the experience of a large part of the female population, support profitable industries that rely on the worries and concerns that individual women feel about their health, their appearance and their social relations. The world of Helen Fielding's fictional young woman Bridget Jones is in all senses a world which offers many possibilities of profit. This is not just about the value of the character to her author, but about the validation of Bridget's worries to the many institutions that depend upon them. Bridget Jones might well be a lovable fictional character, but the very fact of that sympathy for her makes it easier for readers to identify with her insecurities and, through that, accept them as part of the 'ordinary' world. Worries about body weight, one of the issues that concerns Bridget Jones, are just one example of the ways in which concern can be easily translated by a wish to buy the goods and services that might solve the problem.

We might also note that concerns about body weight increased considerably throughout the twentieth century. But women today are 'battling' with it (in that usual neo-military language employed about everything to do with the body, from overweight to cancer), and in doing so providing fertile ground for expensive remedies. This is just one example of the way in which the body, especially the female body, has become such a bottomless pit of worry and concern for each and every one of us. There is very little escape from concern about the body in most of the urbanized world, since its representation is as omnipresent as the facilities for various forms of its modification and 'improvement'. These exist side by side with the very circumstances that are likely to produce the imperfect body: a sedentary existence and food that is saturated with sugar. Couple this with the daily suggestion that physical perfection is an essential part of that Protestant mission to create a world in which work may, for some, provide salvation. So we are not just encouraged to work hard through our bodies; we have to work hard *on* them. We do not need the Calvinist elders of sixteenth-century Geneva to police us; we have the *Daily Mail*, *People* magazine and endless other forms of the surveillance of the body. These various sources all ensure that any departure from a state of perfection will be immediately noticed and policed. We may be aware of the many problems of this form of policing, but it is very difficult for individuals to escape both the self-policing and the policing of others that are the consequence of the daily barrage of body assessment that is part both of the literal urban world and of the more fictitious world of the internet.

Gender inequality, in the urban worlds which have become, and are becoming, the universal place of twenty-first-century existence, is, at present, unlikely to diminish. In this context we should not expect feminist energy and protest to diminish; it is impossible that we should not protest about the vilification of women in the media or the many different forms of the global exploitation of women. But we also have to recognize three fundamental aspects of gender inequality. The first is that rage and fury about the wilful degradation of the female are not a feature only of the twenty-first century; nor are they to be approached through the conventional lens of a 'moral panic'. Of course it is appalling that women and their bodies should be abused, but what is crucial here is that we recognize the motives for this, motives that do not lie solely in psychoanalytical discourses about, for example, the 'fear' of the feminine. In this, we also have to be aware of the limitations of reaching for psychoanalytical explanations for gender inequality. The powerful readings that psychoanalysis makes possible of individual cases, be they individual human beings or individual texts, can become less convincing when applied to collective groups of human beings, divided as they often are by class and race. At the same time, reaching for explanations that in a sense 'individualize' historical periods – to write, for example, of 'the Victorians' – obscures not only much of the social variation within those periods, but also the ways in which it is all too easy to impose on both the present and the past our historically based projections from our own situation. For example, in a letter to the *Guardian* newspaper in 2014, Christopher Prendergast effectively demonstrated the dangerous weight of fantasies about the past. Writing about the policies of the then British secretary of state for education, Michael Gove, Prendergast described him as 'a man lost in translation between past and present, and more precisely the fantasy, bordering on obsession, of the arriviste'.[15]

What does run as a constant through the past centuries is that people have to provide for the material existence of themselves and their dependents. This apparently obvious aspect of human existence is often obscured, or only regarded as significant in terms of the global south; 'we' have to 'develop' countries outside the west which struggle with different forms and levels of poverty. This dynamic obscures two important issues: the long-term destabilization and exploitation of the global south by the global north, and the implicit assumption that western poverty is somehow an aberrant aspect of our way of life, and not one that has a structural relationship to other forms of poverty. It is not that the global north was the only disruptive force in the global south, whose societies were just as often at war with one another as any in the global north. But the picture of itself which the west often projects, and which has an impact on how we think about gender inequality, is that the very form of our social relationships are in some sense different from others. It is therefore all too easy for feminism to ignore collective, structural forms of inequality and to turn both to individual solutions and to interventions about the 'discourse' of gender. In this way, arguments about gender inequality become arguments about changing the 'attitudes' or the 'aspirations' of women, liberal engagements which historically have done little to change the order of relations between classes and races in the global north.

Any engagement with gender inequality must recognize that liberalism is not enough. There is no doubt that liberal policies about sexual behaviour, throughout the world, have changed for the better the lives of millions of people. But the forms of liberalism which are articulated through changes to legislation should be distinguished from those which support the view that social inequality can be confronted, changed and diminished through various forms of institutional modification, most particularly that of education. We have to recognize that, whilst the education available to all citizens of the west has been extended and enlarged in the past hundred years, social inequality not only persists but, as already noted, is increasing. This is not necessarily because forms of education are at fault (although far too many people take the view that all sectors of education should be more closely linked to the needs and concerns of the labour market, and are encouraging programmes to make education more directly 'relevant' to employment), but because the world of employment is changing and the number of well-paid, secure jobs is decreasing. The recognition of those new circumstances is fundamental to any – not just feminist – account of social inequality. So here lies an example of the way in which feminism can be distracted by questions about the number of women who are professionally 'successful' in whatever the context is, and in doing so can fail to recognize that the very context in which we work is changing. For example, studies of the number of women in academia who reach senior positions rightly identifies the difficulties which women academics face, whilst often failing to emphasize both the growing casualization and the growing internal divisions of the system.[16] Both these latter characteristics have implications not just for gender but also for class and race relations.

No study of gender inequality would be complete without two further comments: on the wider social consequences of the connections between gender and social inequality, and suggestions for a way forward. In terms of the connections between social inequality and gender inequality, we have to recognize two things. First, working life is becoming more insecure for more people and is constitutive of forms of often violent competition between both individuals and groups. Second, our determined pursuit of highly gendered and often sexualized forms of competition – for jobs, money, liveable urban space – occur within persisting patriarchal fantasies about what women should be, which support both individuals and institutions. There are therefore not only individual acts of violence against women but also forms of state violence. The first such form is the refusal of many states to recognize the world of everyday responsibilities shouldered by all adults, and the ways in which this responsibility is both gendered and lessened or increased by degrees of social privilege. The second is the extraordinary violence of both individuals and states in response to public acts of minor forms of female subversion: an irreverent song in a Russian church provokes furious repercussions, just as the demand for the display of the portrait of a long-dead woman writer on banknotes leads to death threats. Third, and finally, violence against women in conflict and war continues. These instances suggest not only the continuation of ancient fears about the disruption of the gender order, but also the fragile confidence of those in power.[17]

The question of what is to be done has to start with the abandonment of fantasies about emancipation and progress. We have to refuse to accept dramatic or sensational accounts of the achievement of gender equality, particularly those which focus on the achievements of individual women, accounts which are in their own way often more supportive of existing social relations than critical of them. Here, it is explicitly not expected that more women in various kinds of elites will transform the social world, or that, for example, more available child care is in itself transformative of the conditions and rewards of paid work, or that new forms of sexual citizenship will provide the basis for new forms of democracy. Without endorsing the sentiments that led George Eliot, at the conclusion of her novel *Middlemarch*, to suggest that 'the growing good of the world is partly dependent on unhistoric acts', we have to recognize the political implications of the conditions of existence of those who, as Eliot wrote, 'lived faithfully a hidden life'.[18] Those faithful, hidden lives of women demand a social and political value; it cannot remain taken for granted that the work of care for others remains absent from the political agenda, not specifically because this work has always been largely the work of women, but because without a politics that addresses the social relationships of care there is no such thing as a civilized society. The twenty-first century encourages us all towards exceptionalism, individualism and the deep hunger for the extraordinary, all of which maintain various forms of inequality. No creature, as Eliot wrote in the same context, 'is so strong that it is not greatly determined by what lies outside it'. Without the recognition of the universal human experience of being born into conditions of social inequality, in cultures of often rampant individualism, we will never be able to recognize, let alone address, inequalities of gender. In a century which shows all the signs of increasing forms of social inequality and the exploitation of the world's resources, both human and natural, we have to see that gender inequality is not some special kind of inequality, or a matter of personal choices about sexual identity, but a constitutive part of that very universal inequality. Whether we speak of the politics of social reproduction or of everyday life, we need to address the gendered ways in which these constitutive parts of all our lives are maintained.

Notes

Preface

1 Laura Bates, *Everyday Sexism*.
2 Beatrix Campbell, *End of Equality*, p. 7.
3 Luc Boltanski and Eve Chiapello, 'The Role of Criticism in the Dynamics of Capitalism'.

Chapter 1 What is Gender Inequality?

1 Kimberlé Crenshaw, 'Mapping the Margins'.
2 This point was made by Pankaj Mishra in the *Guardian*, 20 January 2015.
3 Edward Said, *Reflections on Exile and Other Literary and Cultural Essays*, p. xxv.
4 Danny Dorling, *Inequality and the 1%*.
5 Ruth Pearson and Diane Elson, 'Transcending the Impact of the Financial Crisis in the United Kingdom'.
6 Although what Pearson and Elson discuss is specifically the British case, similar patterns of the impact of financial austerity on women could be found elsewhere in Europe and the United States, for example in Tom Clark, *Hard Times*, pp. 60-1. A vivid account of the lives

of people in the USA affected by 'austerity' is Linda Tirado, *Hand to Mouth*; for the UK similarly vivid accounts are given in Jeremy Seabrook, *Pauperland*, pp. 153–88, and Lisa McKenzie, *Getting B*. For the political transformation that might transform social inequality, see Zoe Williams, *Get it Together*.

7 Jacqueline Rose, *Women in Dark Times*, p. ix..
8 See: Laura Bates, *Everyday Sexism*; Laurie Penny, *Unspeakable Things*.
9 Joseph Stiglitz, 'The Global Crisis, Social Protection and Jobs'; Anthony Atkinson, *Inequality*; Thomas Piketty, *Capital*; Danny Dorling, *Injustice*; Ha-Joon Chang, *23 Things They Didn't Tell You About Capitalism*; Kate Pickett and Richard Wilkinson, *The Spirit Level*. When Dorling does mention gender he takes a positive view of the ways in which greater educational opportunities for women, and a lower birth rate, are creating a situation in which our class system is beginning to change. Danny Dorling, 'Thinking about Class'.
10 See, amongst others: D. Harvey, 'Afterthoughts on Piketty's *Capital*', Y. Varoufakis, 'Egalitarianism's Latest Foe'.
11 The unpaid and unrecognized work of both care and work in the household economy that women perform has long been a central issue in feminist politics. See: Margaret Reid, *The Economics of Household Production* and 'The Economic Contribution of Homemakers'; Selma James, *Sex, Race and Class*; and Mariarosa Dalla Costa and Selma James, *The Power of Women and the Subversion of the Community*.
12 Adam Smith, *The Wealth of Nations*, pp. 429–30.
13 Katrine Marçal, *Who Cooked Adam Smith's Dinner?*
14 Simone de Beauvoir, *The Second Sex*, pp. 484-91.
15 Charles Moore, *Margaret Thatcher: The Authorised Biography. Vol. 1* and *Vol. 2*.
16 Eric Hobsbawm, 'The Social Revolution'.
17 The strikes of 1903 in garment factories in New York had been preceded in 1857 by similar strikes. At the time of the 1903 strikes a New York magistrate had asserted that 'the strikes were a strike against God'. This provoked George Bernard Shaw to send a telegram to the strikers saying, 'Delightful. Medieval America always in intimate personal contact with the Almighty.'
18 For the quotation by Jayaben Desai see Striking Women, 'Striking Out'. For further discussions see Amrit Wilson, *Finding a Voice*, and Nicola Charles, 'Women and Trade Unions in the Workplace'.

19 Mary Astell, *A Serious Proposal to the Ladies*, pp. 7–8.

20 The Women's Library at the London School of Economics contains two sets of papers related to the assisted emigration of middle-class women in the nineteenth century: Anon., 'The Female Middle Class Emigration Society, 1862-1885' and 'The British Women's Emigration Society, 1885-1919'.

21 Coventry Patmore's poem told of the various doubts and uncertainties of two married couples, problems eventually resolved in conjugal certainty and harmony.

22 Emma Goldman, *Anarchism and other Essays*, p. 224.

23 Hermione Lee, *Virginia Woolf*, p. 693.

24 Linda McDowell, *Capital Culture*.

25 Kristen Schilt, *Just One of the Guys*.

26 Adrienne Rich, 'Compulsory Heterosexuality and Lesbian Experience'.

27 The Women's Budget Group and the Fawcett Society are the two best-known sources of information about gender inequality in the UK. Other relevant sources for international material are discussed in Ania Plomien, 'Economy'. For the USA see Colette Morrow and Terri Ann Frederick, *Getting In Is Not Enough*. A detailed discussion of the links between class and gender inequality on both sides of the Atlantic is provided in *Gender-Class Equality in Political Economies* by Lynn Prince Cooks.

28 See L. Nousiainen et al., 'Theorising Gender Equality', and P. Kettunen, 'Reinterpreting the Historicity of the Nordic Model'.

29 Daniel Stedman Jones, *Masters of the Universe*, p. 344.

30 See 'Mike Savage, 'The "Class Ceiling" and the New Class War', and further discussion from the book from which this article was drawn: Mike Savage, *Social Class in the 21st Century*, pp. 361-88.

31 Barbara Taylor, *The Last Asylum*, p. 82.

32 Sheryl Sandberg, *Lean In*.

33 Dawn Foster, *Lean Out*, and Elizabeth Bruenig, 'Sheryl Sandberg's Lean in Philosophy Doesn't Just Ignore Disadvantaged Women'.

34 Alison Wolf, *The XX Factor*, and Hanna Rosin, *The End of Men*.

35 Sheryl Sandberg, *Lean In*, p. 10.

36 Zygmunt Bauman, *Liquid Modernity*. The gendered impact of the 'disorder' of modernity is discussed in Louise Wattis and Liz James, 'Exploring Order and Disorder'.

37 Anne-Marie Slaughter, *Unfinished Business*.
38 Richard Yates, *Revolutionary Road*; Evan S. Connell, *Mrs Bridge*; Betty Friedan, *The Feminine Mystique*; Sylvia Plath, *The Bell Jar*.
39 Tana French, *Broken Harbour*.
40 Lauren Berlant, *Cruel Optimism*.
41 Michael Lewis, *The Big Short*.
42 Georg Simmel, 'Spatial and Urban Culture', p. 143.

Chapter 2 Worlds of Inequality

1 See Tracey Rosenberg, 'The Awkward Blot', and Ross Murfin, 'Novel Representations'.
2 Mirra Komarovsky, 'Cultural Contradictions and Sex Roles'.
3 Karl Marx, *Capital. Vol. 1*, p. 254.
4 The building had major construction faults and had never been intended as a factory.
5 The longevity of appalling working conditions and 'slum cities' is discussed in Mike Davis, *Planet Slums*.
6 See International Labour Organisation, *Deadly Secrets*, and War on Want, 'Never Again: Making Fashion's Factories Safe'.
7 Suroopa Mukherjee, *Surviving Bhopal*.
8 Suroopa Mukherjee, *Surviving Bhopal*, p. 19.
9 Suroopa Mukherjee, *Surviving Bhopal*, p. 182.
10 On these various issues see Jane Humphries, *Childhood and Child Labour in the British Industrial Revolution*, and P. Griffin, 'The Gendered Global Political Economy'.
11 Kalpana Wilson, '"Race", Gender and Neo-liberalism', and Lisa Rofel, *Desiring China*.
12 See Anon., 'Interview with Terence Conran'.
13 The debates in the UK in the early nineteenth century about earnings are discussed in Barbara Taylor, *Eve and the New Jerusalem*, pp. 108–10. One important point that emerges from Taylor's work is that in some families the main earner was the wife rather than the husband.
14 One household in which relations with the servants produced various tensions was that of Leonard and Virginia Woolf. See Alison Light, *Mrs Woolf and the Servants*. The reality of life as a servant is explored in Lucy Delap, *Knowing their Place*.

15 On the history of women in the workforce in the UK see Sally Alexander, 'Becoming a Woman in London in the 1920s and 1930s', and Jane Lewis, *Women in England, 1870-1950.* On the USA see Louise A. Tilly and Joan W. Scott, *Women, Work and Family.*

16 In terms of paid parental leave, the United States is alone amongst rich countries in not providing any state support; as Tara Siegel Bernard remarked in 'In Paid Family Leave, U.S. Trails Most of the Globe.' In the UK, from October 2011 lone parents have had to take a job or be actively seeking one from the time when their youngest child is five years old, or lose 40 per cent of their benefits.

17 In April 2011, David Willetts, the then minister with responsibility for higher education in the UK coalition government, expressed the view that middle-class women had taken away jobs from 'bright' working-class boys. See Hélène Mulholland, 'David Willetts blames feminism over lack of jobs for working men'.

18 Helma Lutz, *The New Maids*, p. 20.

19 Isabella Acevedo was deported to Colombia in July 2014. The laws surrounding prostitution are contentious: the proposal to criminalize paying for sex in England and Wales (that is, to adopt what is known as the 'Nordic Model', the law applying to Norway, Sweden and Iceland) was not accepted in England despite support from the 'End Demand' campaign. However, it is a criminal offence in England and Wales to pay for sex with a person who has been subjected to force, and this is a 'strict liability' offence, that is, ignorance of the situation of the prostitute does not constitute a defence.

20 Sumi Madhok et al., *Gender, Agency, Coercion*, pp. 2-3.

21 For austerity policies' impact on the health (emotional and physical) of individuals see David Stuckler and Basu Sanjay, *The Body Economic.*

22 Barbara Einhorn, *Cinderella Goes to Market.*

23 The evidence about the impact of marketization in the old Soviet Union is often contradictory. For example, Judy Dempsey, 'Study Looks at Mortality in Post-Soviet Era', argued in January 2009 that since 1989 life expectancy had been dramatically reduced.

24 The book in question is called *My Parents Open Carry* by Brian Jeffs and Nathan Nephew. When the book was published buyers were promised a free copy of *Raising Boys Feminists Will Hate* by Douglas Giles.

25 A revised edition was published in 2010 as *The Spirit Level: Why Equality is Better for Everyone*.

26 See Toru Yamamori, 'A Feminist Way to Unconditional Basic Income'.

27 For recent discussions about violence against women see Nandi Mkhize, 'Violence Against Women', and UN, 'Facts and Figures'.

28 Anthony Giddens, *The Transformation of Intimacy*.

29 Simone de Beauvoir, *The Prime of Life*, p. 193.

30 Julia Bush, *Women against the Vote*.

31 The UK charity Grandparents Plus estimated that in the UK one in four families is dependent on grandparents for child care. See Grandparents Plus, 'Grandparents Throw Squeezed Families a Life Line'.

32 A pre-austerity account of the organization of families across Europe is given in the essays in Jane Lewis, *Children, Changing Families and Welfare States*.

33 The classic article on women as a 'reserve army' is Irene Bruegel, 'Women as a Reserve Army of Labour'.

34 Richard Hoggart, *The Uses of Literacy*, p. 169.

Chapter 3 Problems of Subjectivity

1 One example of the part played by men in the politics of abortion was that of the MP David Steel, who piloted the 1967 Abortion Act through the House of Commons. In the USA the definitive Supreme Court judgement was that of *Roe v. Wade* in 1973.

2 Zygmunt Bauman, *Liquid Love*, and Herbert Marcuse, *Eros and Civilisation*.

3 Michel Foucault, 'Space, Knowledge and Power'.

4 Simone de Beauvoir, *Old Age*, and Lynne Segal, *Out of Time*. The intersection of ageing and different forms of sexuality is discussed in Jon Binnie and Christian Klesse, 'The Politics of Age, Temporality and Intergenerationality in Transnational Lesbian, Gay, Bisexual, Transgender and Queer Activist Networks'.

5 Susan Bordo, *Unbearable Weight*.

6 At the time of writing, a generally accepted figure for the UK of the number of people suffering from anorexia was 1.6 million, of whom 10 per cent were boys. The question of 'fat' has long been a

feminist issue, most famously stated in Susie Orbach's *Fat Is a Feminist Issue*.

7 In 2014 the annual turnover of 'the beauty industry', a somewhat imprecise category, was estimated at £17 billion, with an expected growth of 16 per cent by 2016 (Beatrice Aidin, 'Business Face of UK Beauty'). In the same article in which these figures were quoted it was also said that the 'beauty' industry was 'recession proof'.

8 See Laurie Penny, *Meat Market*.

9 A two-part television film about the circumstances and the outcome of false accusations of murder against Christopher Jeffries, *The Lost Honour of Christopher Jeffries* (written by Peter Morgan), was shown on ITV in 2014. The suspicion surrounding 'loneliness' in detective fiction is discussed in Tina Mantymaki, 'Women who Kill Men'.

10 Adrienne Rich, 'Compulsory Heterosexuality and Lesbian Experience'.

11 Gillian Rose, *Love's Work*, p. 127.

12 Debates on sexualization are discussed in R. Danielle Egan, *Becoming Sexual*.

13 Zygmunt Bauman, *Liquid Love*, p. 49.

14 David Frisby and Mike Featherstone, *Simmel on Culture*, p. 192.

15 Lauren Berlant, *Cruel Optimism*.

16 Simone de Beauvoir, *The Prime of Life*, p. 77.

17 Judith Butler, *Frames of War*, pp. 1–33.

18 Mike Savage et al., 'A New Model of Social Class?', p. 245. In this article, Savage and his colleagues estimate that 15 per cent of the UK population can de defined in terms of a 'precariat'; namely those with no significant social or material resources.

19 Michel Foucault, quoted in Barry Smart, *Michel Foucault*, p. 98.

20 David Macey's *The Lives of Michel Foucault*, pp. 173 and 345, records instances of the hostility of their relationship.

21 Jacqueline Rose, *Women in Dark Times*, p. 55.

22 Clare Hemmings, 'Sexual Passion and the Promise of Revolution'.

23 Rosa Luxemburg, *Reform or Revolution and Other Writings*, p. 121.

24 Martha Nussbaum, *Political Emotion*.

25 Sherry B. Ortner, 'Is Female to Male as Nature is to Culture?'.

26 Ulrich Beck and Elisabeth Beck-Gernsheim, *The Normal Chaos of Love*.

27 Max Weber, *From Max Weber: Essays*, p. 347.

28 Elizabeth Wilson, *Adorned in Dreams*.
29 See Mary Beard, 'The Public Voice of Women'. Laura Bates, the author of *Everyday Sexism* and a contributor to the New York-based project 'Women under Siege', founded the Everyday Sexism Project to catalogue day-to-day instances of sexism. Laurie Penny has documented the negative impact of the internet on women in *Cybersexism*.
30 See 'Introduction' in Juliet Mitchell, *The Selected Melanie Klein*, pp. 9–34.
31 Henrietta Moore, *The Subject of Anthropology*.
32 Gilles Deleuze and Félix Guattari, 'Section 2: Psychoanalysis and Familialism: The Holy Family'.
33 Gilles Deleuze and Félix Guattari, 'Section 2: Psychoanalysis and Familialism: The Holy Family', p. 141.
34 Karl Marx and Frederick Engels, *The Holy Family, or Critique of Critical Criticism*.
35 Raewyn Connell, *Masculinities*.
36 See Rahila Gupta, 'Transgender'.
37 Anne Olivier Bell, *The Diary of Virginia Bell. Vol. One*, p. 75.
38 Max Weber, *The Protestant Ethic and the Spirit of Capitalism*, p. 181.

Chapter 4 Enter Feminism

1 Edward Higgs, 'The Rise of the Information State'.
2 The classic work on the crowd is George Rude's *The Crowd in History*. For examples of the discussion of Rude's work see Andrew Charlesworth, 'George Rude and the Anatomy of the Crowd'.
3 Katherine Connelly, *Sylvia Pankhurst*, p. 35.
4 The term 'hysteria' has been claimed for general use by Juliet Mitchell in *Mad Men and Medusas*.
5 Margery Spring Rice, *Working Class Wives*, p. 206. The book was first published in 1939. Anna Davin's article 'Imperialism and Motherhood' was published in 1978.
6 Alexandra Harris, *Romantic Moderns*.
7 Simone de Beauvoir, *Force of Circumstance*.
8 Amongst the now considerable literature on Beauvoir see Penelope Deutscher, *The Philosophy of Simone de Beauvoir*; Sonia Kruks, *Simone*

de Beauvoir and the Politics of Ambiguity; and Toril Moi, *Simone de Beauvoir*.

9 Simone de Beauvoir, *Force of Circumstance*, p. 94.

10 Simone de Beauvoir, *The Prime of Life*, p. 589.

11 Margaret Walters, 'The Rights and Wrongs of Women'.

12 Amal Treacher Kabesh, *Postcolonial Masculinities*.

13 Firestone dedicated her book to Simone de Beauvoir, 'who', she writes, 'has endured'. A further discussion of this book can be found in Mandy Merck and Stella Sandford, *Further Adventures of the Dialectic of Sex*.

14 Simone de Beauvoir, *Force of Circumstance*, p. 192.

15 Luce Irigaray, *This Sex Which Is Not One* and, more recently, *In the Beginning She Was*. Monique Wittig, *Les Guérillères* and *The Straight Mind and Other Essays*.

16 Karl Marx, 'The Eighteenth Brumaire of Louis Bonaparte, p. 246.

17 Walter Benjamin, 'Theses on the Philosophy of History, IX', p. 259.

18 Viola Klein, *The Feminine Character*.

19 Viola Klein and Alva Myrdal, *Women's Two Roles*.

20 See the discussion in Dorothy Sue Cobble et al., *A Short, Surprising History of American Women's Movements*, pp. 107-11.

21 The brilliant and important work of Raphael Samuel is to be found in two collections of his work: *Theatres of Memory* and *Island Stories*.

22 Ayse Parla, '"The Honour" of the State'. Protests against the Erdoğan government in Turkey, and its conservative social policies, have been discussed in Erdem Yörük and Murat Yüksel, 'Turkey's Hot Summer'.

23 Andrea Dworkin, *Pornography* and *Intercourse*, and Catharine MacKinnon, *Are Women Human?*

24 Caroline Criado-Perez campaigned successfully to have the picture of Jane Austen on an English £10 note, as a result of which she received death and rape threats. In January 2014 John Nimmo and Isabella Sorley were both sentenced to terms of imprisonment (8 weeks and 12 weeks respectively) for their Twitter threats against Criado-Perez. See her book *Do It Like a Woman*.

25 Frances Mary Buss, *Leaves from the Notebooks of Frances M. Buss*.

26 The classic statement of the conservatism/Conservative voting of women in the UK was voiced in Jean Blondel's *Voters, Parties and Leaders*.

27 Some of that dissent and dissatisfaction is described in Virginia Nicholson, *Perfect Wives in Ideal Homes*.

28 The advertising slogan 'You've come a long way, baby' was first used for Virginia Slims cigarettes in 1978. It pictured a glamorous young woman against a background of various forms of female experience in the past . . . all of which were less than glamorous.

29 A T-shirt with the slogan 'This what a feminist looks like' was launched by the UK Fawcett Society in October 2014. Discussion followed about the factory conditions in which the T-shirt was produced. See www.fawcettsociety.org.uk/feminist-looks-like-t-shirt-fawcett-society-response, November 2014.

30 Adlai Stevenson, at the Commencement ceremony at Smith College in the US in 1955, spoke of women's responsibility to 'frustrate the evils of [the] vocational specialization' of contemporary society. The role of educated wives was to keep men 'whole'.

31 The suffragette poster with the slogans 'What a woman may be and yet not have the vote' and 'What a man may have been and not lose the vote', can be seen at www.museumoflondonprints.com.

32 Joan Wallach Scott, *The Fantasy of Feminist History*, p. 43.

33 Jeffrey Weeks, *Sex, Politics and Society*.

34 Owen Jones, *The Establishment*); Naomi Klein, *This Changes Everything*; Michael Moore, director of (amongst other films): *Bowling for Columbine* (2002), *Capitalism : A Love Story* (2009) and *Where to Invade Next ?* (2015).

35 George Grosz was a member of the Spartacist League and a passionate critic of German militarism and Nazism. He left Germany in 1933 for the USA but returned to Germany after the end of the Second World War.

36 Sara Ahmed, *The Promise of Happiness*; Lauren Berlant, *Cruel Optimism*; Arlie Hochschild, *The Managed Heart*.

37 Eve Kosofsky Sedgwick, *Between Men* and *Epistemology of the Closet*.

38 Rachel Holmes, *Eleanor Marx*, p. 259.

39 Rachel Holmes, *Eleanor Marx*, p. 261.

40 Katherine Connelly, *Sylvia Pankhurst*, p. 46.

41 John Davis, *People of the Mediterranean*, p. 168.

42 See the classic statement about the state's view of the responsibilities of women: Hilary Land, 'The Family Wage'.

43 The academic literature on law is now considerable. See the following

for a discussion of some of the key issues: C. Wells, 'The Impact of Feminist Thinking on Criminal Law and Justice' (on English law in general); V. Munro, 'Sexual Autonomy' (on sexual violence and constructions of womanhood in English law); for a global perspective see Rashida Manjoo, *Violence against Women*.

44 Thomas Kuhn, *The Structure of Scientific Revolutions*.

45 Ann Oakley, *From Here to Maternity* and *Housewife*; Hannah Gavron, *The Captive Wife*.

46 C.W. Mills, *White Collar* and *The Power Elite*; Marie Jahoda et al., *Marienthal*.

47 Laurie Penny, *Unspeakable Things*, p. 153.

48 Laurie Penny, *Unspeakable Things*, p. 173.

49 The terror of downward social mobility in the USA was described by Barbara Ehrenreich in *Fear of Falling*. The web is at present full of advice on how to manage the 'stress' of paid work; almost all of it assigns responsibility for managing stress to the employee.

50 The stage play of *The Vagina Monologues* took its title from the book of the same name by Eve Ensler.

51 John Jervis, *Sensational Subjects*, p. 7.

52 Hanna Rosin, *The End of Men*; Lynne Segal, *Is the Future Female?*

53 Kristen Schilt and Lauren Westbrook, 'Doing Gender, Determining Gender'.

54 See arguments against paternity leave in Jon Gunnarsson, 'Against Parental Leave', and for resistance by women to women's suffrage see Jane Camhi, *Women against Women*, for the United States, and Julia Bush, *Women against the Vote*, for the UK.

55 Amy Chua, *Battle Hymn of the Tiger Mother*.

56 Mark Carney, 'Inclusive Capitalism'.

Chapter 5 Making Gender Equality

1 S.M. Cretney, '"What Will the Women Want Next?"'.

2 Jacqueline Rose, 'We Need a Bold, Scandalous Feminism'.

3 Diane Reay, 'Beyond Consciousness?', and other articles in the same volume examine links between class, gender, race and education in both Britain and the USA.

4 The complexities of political loyalties and party politics about the passing of the UK Child Benefit Act in 1979 are given in

Oonagh Grey and Richard Cracknell, *Women in Parliament*, pp. 25-6.

5 On the history of women in the UK workforce see Sally Alexander, *Becoming a Woman*; Jane Lewis, *Women in England, 1870-1950*. On the USA see Louise A. Tilly and Joan W. Scott, *Women, Work and Family*.

6 Gramsci, *Prison Notebooks*, letter of 19[h] December 1929.

7 Nigella Lawson, *How To Be a Domestic Goddess*.

8 Raphael Samuel, 'Retrochic', in Raphael Samuel, *Theatres of Memory*, pp. 83-118.

9 Clara Fischer, 'Gender, Nation and the Politics of Shame'; Emma Casey, '"Catalogue Communities"'; Imogen Tyler, *Revolting Subjects*.

10 Kari Melby et al., *Gender Equality and Welfare Politics in Scandinavia*.

11 See, for canonical contributions to this genre, Carolyn Steedman, *Landscape for a Good Woman*, and Lorna Sage, *Bad Blood*.

12 Defoe, *Moll Flanders*, p. 23.

13 See Graeme Maxton, 'Economic Growth doesn't Create Jobs, It Destroys Them', and the various publications of the Foundation for the Economics of Sustainability, www.feasta.org.

14 Lisa Rofel, *Desiring China*.

15 Professor Christopher Prendergast, Letter to the *Guardian*.

16 See Miriam David, *Feminism, Gender and Universities*.

17 See Jane Parpart and Kevin Partridge, 'Soldiering On–'.

18 George Eliot, *Middlemarch*, p. 924.

Bibliography

Ahmed, Sara, *The Promise of Happiness* (Durham, NC, Duke University Press, 2010).

Aidin, Beatrice, 'Business Face of UK Beauty', *The Times*, 4 September 2014, http://raconteur.net/lifestyle/business-face-of-uk-beauty.

Alexander, Sally, *Becoming a Woman: And Other Essays in 19th and 20th Century Feminist History* (London, Virago, 1994).

Alexander, Sally, 'Becoming a Woman in London in the 1920s and 1930s', in Sally Alexander, *Becoming a Woman: And Other Essays in 19th and 20th Century Feminist History* (London, Virago, 1994), 203–24.

Anon., 'The British Women's Emigration Society, 1885–1919', Women's Library, London School of Economics.

Anon., 'The Female Middle Class Emigration Society, 1862–1885', Women's Library, London School of Economics.

Anon., 'Interview with Terence Conran', *Independent*, 4 July 1997.

Anon. ('Sophia'), 'Woman Not Inferior to Man: or, a Short and Modest Vindication of the Natural Right of the Fair-Sex to a Perfect Equality of Power, Dignity and Esteem with the Men' (London: Printed for John Hawkins, 1739).

Arendt, Hannah, 'Labor v. Work', in Hannah Arendt, *The Human Condition* (Chicago, University of Chicago Press, 1958), 79–135.

Astell, Mary, *A Serious Proposal to the Ladies*, first published 1694 (London, Pickering and Chatto, 1997).

Atkinson, Anthony, *Inequality* (Cambridge, MA, Harvard University Press, 2015).

Bates, Laura, *Everyday Sexism* (London, Simon and Schuster, 2014).

Bauman, Zygmunt, *Liquid Love: On the Frailty of Human Bonds* (Cambridge and New York, Polity, 2003).

Bauman, Zygmunt, *Liquid Modernity* (Cambridge, Polity 2000).

Beard, Mary, 'The Public Voice of Women', *London Review of Books*, 36/6 (2014), 11–14.

Beck, Ulrich and Elisabeth Beck-Gernsheim, *The Normal Chaos of Love* (Cambridge and Malden, MA, Polity, 1995).

Benjamin, Walter, 'Theses on the Philosophy of History, IX', in Walter Benjamin, *Illuminations* (London, Jonathan Cape, 1950), 255–66.

Berlant, Lauren, *Cruel Optimism* (Durham, NC, Duke University Press, 2011).

Bernard, Tara Siegel, 'In Paid Family Leave, U.S. Trails Most of the Globe, *New York Times*, 22 February 2013, http://www.nytimes. com/2013/02/23/your-money/us-trails-much-of-the-world-in-pro viding-paid-family-leave.html?_r=0.

Binnie, Jon and Christian Klesse, 'The Politics of Age, Temporality and Intergenerationality in Transnational Lesbian, Gay, Bisexual, Transgender and Queer Activist Networks', *Sociology*, 47/3 (2012), 580–95.

Blondel, Jean, *Voters, Parties and Leaders: The Social Fabric of British Politics* (Harmondsworth, Penguin, 1963).

Boltanski, Luc and Eve Chiapello, 'The Role of Criticism in the Dynamics of Capitalism', in Max Miller (ed.) *Worlds of Capitalism* (New York and London, Routledge, 2005), 229–58.

Bordo, Susan, *Unbearable Weight* (Los Angeles, University of California Press, 1993).

Bruegel, Irene, 'Women as a Reserve Army of Labour: A Note on Recent British Experience', *Feminist Review*, 3 (1979), 12–23.

Bruenig, Elizabeth, 'Sheryl Sandberg's Lean in Philosophy Doesn't Just Ignore Disadvantaged Women. It Hurts Their Cause', 9 March 2015, https://newrepublic.com/article/121249/sheryl-sandbergs-lean-femi nism-puts-women-issues-risk.

Bush, Julia, *Women against the Vote: Female Anti-Suffragism in Britain* (Oxford, Oxford University Press, 2007).

Buss, Frances Mary, *Leaves from the Notebooks of Frances M. Buss* (London and New York, Macmillan, 1896).

Butler, Judith, *Frames of War: When is Life Grievable?* (London and New York, Verso, 2009).

Camhi, Jane, *Women against Women: American Anti-Suffragism, 1880–1920* (Brooklyn, Carlson Press, 1994).

Campbell, Beatrix, *End of Equality* (London, New York and Calcutta, Seagull Books, 2013).

Carney, Mark, 'Inclusive Capitalism: Creating a Sense of the Systemic', speech given by Mark Carney, governor of the Bank of England, at the Conference on Inclusive Capitalism, London, 27 May 2014, http://www.bankofengland.co.uk/publications/Documents/speeches/2014/speech731.pdf.

Casey, Emma, ' "Catalogue Communities": Work and Consumption in the Catalogue Industry', *Journal of Consumer Culture*, 15/3 (2015), 391–406.

Chang, Ha-Joon, *23 Things They Didn't Tell You About Capitalism* (London and New York, Penguin, 2010).

Charles, Nicola, 'Women and Trade Unions in the Workplace', *Feminist Review*, 15 (1983), 3–22.

Charlesworth, Andrew, 'George Rude and the Anatomy of the Crowd', *Labour History Review*, 55/3 (1990), 27–46.

Chomsky, Noam, *Occupy* (London, Penguin, 2012).

Chua, Amy, *Battle Hymn of the Tiger Mother* (London, Bloomsbury, 2012).

Clark, Tom, *Hard Times* (New Haven, Yale University Press, 2015).

Cobble, Dorothy Sue, Linda Gordon and Astrid Henry (eds.), *A Short, Surprising History of American Women's Movements* (London and New York, W.W. Norton, 2014).

Connell, Evan S., *Mrs Bridge*, first published 1959 (London, Heinemann, 1960).

Connell, Raewyn, *Masculinities*, 2nd edn (Berkeley, University of California Press, 2005).

Connelly, Katherine, *Sylvia Pankhurst: Suffragette, Socialist and Scourge of Empire* (London and New York, Pluto Press, 2013).

Cooks, Lynn Prince, *Gender-Class Equality in Political Economies* (London and New York, Routledge, 2011).

Costa, Mariarosa Dalla and Selma James, *The Power of Women and the Subversion of the Community* (Bristol, Falling Wall Press, 1973).

Crenshaw, Kimberlé, 'Mapping the Margins: Intersectionality, Identity Politics and Violence against Women of Color', *Stanford Law Review*, 43/6 (1991), 1241–99.

Cretney, S.M., ' "What Will the Women Want Next?" The Struggle for Power in the Family, 1925–1975', in S.M. Cretney, *Law Reform and the Family* (Oxford, Oxford University Press, 1998), 155–83.

Criado-Perez, Caroline, *Do It Like a Woman . . . and Change the World* (London, Portobello Books, 2015).

David, Miriam, *Feminism, Gender and Universities: Politics, Passion and Pedagogies* (Farnham, Ashgate, 2014).

Davin, Anna, 'Imperialism and Motherhood', *History Workshop Journal*, 5/1 (1978), 9–66.

Davis, John, *People of the Mediterranean: An Essay in Comparative Anthropology* (London, Routledge and Kegan Paul, 1977).

Davis, Mike, *Planet Slums* (London and New York, Verso, 2006).

de Beauvoir, Simone, *Force of Circumstance* (London, Andre Deutsch, 1965).

de Beauvoir, Simone, *Old Age* (London, Penguin, 1977).

de Beauvoir, Simone, *The Prime of Life* (London, Penguin, 1962).

de Beauvoir, Simone, *The Second Sex* (London, Jonathan Cape, 2009).

Defoe, Daniel, *Moll Flanders*, first published 1722 (London, Pan, 1971).

Delap, Lucy, *Knowing their Place: Domestic Service in Twentieth Century Britain* (Oxford, Oxford University Press, 2011).

Deleuze, Gilles and Félix Guattari, 'Section 2: Psychoanalysis and Familialism: The Holy Family', in Gilles Deleuze and Felix Guattari, *Anti-Oedipus: Capitalism and Schizophrenia* (London, Continuum, 2004), 58–152.

Dempsey, Judy, 'Study Looks at Mortality in Post-Soviet Era', *New York Times*, 16 January 2009, http://www.nytimes.com/2009/01/16/world/europe/16europe.html.

Deutscher, Penelope, *The Philosophy of Simone de Beauvoir: Ambiguity, Conversion, Resistance* (Cambridge and New York, Cambridge University Press, 2008).

Dorling, Danny, *Inequality and the 1%* (London, Verso, 2014).

Dorling, Danny, *Injustice: Why Social Inequality Persists* (Bristol, Policy Press, 2011).

Dorling, Danny, 'Thinking about Class', *Sociology*, 48/3 (2014), 452–62.

Dworkin, Andrea, *Intercourse* (New York, Free Press, 1987).

Dworkin, Andrea, *Pornography: Men Possessing Women* (London, Women's Press, 1981).

Egan, R. Danielle, *Becoming Sexual: A Critical Appraisal of the Sexualisation of Girls* (Malden, MA, and Cambridge, Polity, 2013).

Ehrenreich, Barbara, *Fear of Falling: The Inner Life of the Middle Class* (New York, Harper and Row, 1990).

Einhorn, Barbara, *Cinderella Goes to Market: Citizenship, Gender and Women's Movements in East Central Europe* (London, Verso, 1993).

Eliot, George, *Middlemarch* (Oxford, Oxford University Press, 1999).

Ensler, Eve, *Vagina Monologues*, first published 1998 (Hachette Digital, Little Brown Book Group, 2010).

Faludi, Susan, *Backlash: The Undeclared War Against Women* (London, Chatto and Windus, 1992).

Firestone, Shulamith, *The Dialectic of Sex: The Case for Feminist Revolution* (New York, Bantam Books, 1971).

Fischer, Clara, 'Gender, Nation and the Politics of Shame: Magdalen Laundries and the Institutionalisation of Feminine Transgression in Modern Ireland', https://www.academia.edu/23693456/_Gender_Nation_and_the_Politics_of_Shame_Magdalen_Laundries_and_the_Institutionalisation_of_Feminine_Transgression_in_Modern_Ireland_.

Foster, Dawn, *Lean Out* (London, Repeater, 2016).

Foucault, Michel, 'Space, Knowledge and Power', in Paul Rabinow (ed.) *The Foucault Reader* (New York, Pantheon Press, 1984), 239–56.

Fraser, Nancy, *Fortunes of Feminism: From State-Managed Capitalism to Neoliberal Crisis* (New York, Verso, 2013).

French, Tana, *Broken Harbour* (London, Hodder and Stoughton, 2012).

Friedan, Betty, *The Feminine Mystique* (New York, W.W. Norton, 1963).

Frisby, David and Mike Featherstone (eds.), *Simmel on Culture* (London and Thousand Oaks, CA, Sage, 1997).

Gavron, Hannah, *The Captive Wife: Conflict of Housebound Mothers* (Harmondsworth, Penguin, 1970).

Giddens, Anthony, *The Transformation of Intimacy* (Cambridge, Polity, 1993).

Giles, Douglas, *Raising Boys Feminists Will Hate* (n.p., White Feather Press, 2013).

Goldman, Emma, *Anarchism and other Essays* (New York, Mother Earth Publishing Association, 1910).

Gramsci, Antonio, *Prison Notebooks*, ed. and trans. Quentin Hoare and Geoffrey Nowell Smith (London, Lawrence and Wishart, 1971).

Grandparents Plus, 'Grandparents Throw Squeezed Families a Life Line', http://www.grandparentsplus.org.uk/wp-content/uploads/2013/05/Grandparental-childcare-30-May-2013.pdf.

Greer, Germaine, *The Female Eunuch* (London, McGibbon and Kee, 1970).

Grey, Oonagh and Richard Cracknell (eds.), *Women in Parliament: Making a Difference since 1918* (London, House of Commons Library, 2013).

Griffin, P., 'The Gendered Global Political Economy', in R. Denemark (ed.) *The International Studies Association Compendium* (Oxford, Wiley-Blackwell, 2010), 2631–50.

Gunnarsson, Jon, 'Against Parental Leave', 18 November 2014, http://www.avoiceformen.com/miscellaneous/against-parental-leave.

Gupta, Rahila, 'Transgender: The Challenge to Feminist Politics', https://www.opendemocracy.net/5050/rahila-gupta/transgender-challenge-to-feminist-politics.

Harris, Alexandra, *Romantic Moderns: English Writers, Artists and the Imagination from Virginia Woolf to John Piper* (London, Thames and Hudson, 2010).

Harvey, D., 'Afterthoughts on Piketty's *Capital*', http://davidharvey.org/2014/05.

Hemmings, Clare, 'Sexual Passion and the Promise of Revolution', *Feminist Review*, 106 (2014), 43–59.

Higgs, Edward, 'The Rise of the Information State: The Development of Central State Surveillance of the Citizen in the UK, 1500–2000', *Journal of Historical Sociology*, 14/2 (2001), 175-97.

Hobsbawm, Eric, 'The Social Revolution: 1945–1990' in Eric Hobsbawm, *Age of Extremes* (London and New York, Michael Joseph, 1995), 310–19.

Hochschild, Arlie, *The Managed Heart: Commercialization of Human Feeling* (Berkeley, University of California Press, 2003).

Hoggart, Richard, *The Uses of Literacy* (Harmondsworth, Penguin, 1960).

Holmes, Rachel, *Eleanor Marx: A Life* (London, Bloomsbury, 2014).

Humphries, Jane, *Childhood and Child Labour in the British Industrial Revolution* (Cambridge, Cambridge University Press, 2010).

International Labour Organisation (ILO), *Deadly Secrets* Washington, DC, (International Labour Rights Forum, 2012).

Irigaray, Luce, *In the Beginning She Was* (London and New York, Bloomsbury, 2013).

Irigaray, Luce, *This Sex Which Is Not One*, first published 1977 (English translation: Ithaca, NY, Cornell University Press, 1985).

Jahoda, Marie, Paul Lazarsfeld and Hans Zeisel, *Marienthal: The Sociography of an Unemployed Community*, first published 1933 (New York, Transaction Books, 2002).

James, Selma, *Sex, Race and Class* (Bristol, Falling Wall Press, 1986).

Jeffs, Brian and Nathan Nephew, *My Parents Open Carry* (n.p., White Feather Press, 2014).

Jervis, John, *Sensational Subjects: The Dramatisation of Experience in the Modern World* (London, Bloomsbury, 2015).

Jones, Owen, *The Establishment: And How They Get Away With It* (London, Penguin, 2015).

Kettunen, P., 'Reinterpreting the Historicity of the Nordic Model', *Nordic Journal of Working Life Studies*, 2/4 (2012), 21–43.

Klein, Naomi, *This Changes Everything: Capitalism vs the Climate* (London, Penguin, 2015).

Klein, Viola, *The Feminine Character: History of an Ideology* (London, Routledge and Kegan Paul, 1946).

Klein, Viola and Alva Myrdal, *Women's Two Roles: Home and Work* (London, Routledge and Kegan Paul, 1956).

Komarovsky, Mirra, 'Cultural Contradictions and Sex Roles', *American Journal of Sociology*, 52 (1946), 184–9.

Kosofsky Sedgwick, Eve, *Between Men: English Literature and Male Homosocial Desire* (New York, Columbia University Press, 1993).

Kosofsky Sedgwick, Eve, *Epistemology of the Closet* (Berkeley, University of California Press, 2008).

Kruks, Sonia, *Simone de Beauvoir and the Politics of Ambiguity* (Oxford, Oxford University Press, 2012).

Kuhn, Thomas, *The Structure of Scientific Revolutions* (Chicago, University of Chicago Press, 1962).

Land, Hilary, 'The Family Wage', *New Statesman*, 18 December 1981, 16–18.

Lawson, Nigella, *How to Be a Domestic Goddess: Baking and the Art of Comfort Cooking* (London, Chatto and Windus, 2000).

Lee, Hermione, *Virginia Woolf* (London, Viking, 1997).

Lewis, Jane (ed.), *Children, Changing Families and Welfare States* (Cheltenham, Edward Elgar, 2006).

Lewis, Jane, *Women in England, 1870–1950: Sexual Divisions and Social Change* (Oxford, Wiley, 1985).

Lewis, Michael, *The Big Short* (New York and London, Penguin, 2010).

Light, Alison, *Mrs Woolf and the Servants* (London and New York, Penguin, 2008).

Lutz, Helma, *The New Maids: Transnational Women and the Care Economy* (London and New York, Zed Books, 2011).

Luxemburg, Rosa, *Reform or Revolution and Other Writings* (New York, Dover Books, 2006).

Macey, David, *The Lives of Michel Foucault* (London, Vintage, 1994).

MacKinnon, Catharine, *Are Women Human? And Other International Dialogues* (Cambridge, MA, Harvard University Press, 2006).

Madhok, Sumi, Anne Phillips and Kalpana Wilson (eds.), *Gender, Agency, Coercion* (London and New York, Routledge, 2013).

Manjoo, Rashida, *Violence against Women: Twenty Years of Developments Within the United Nations*, report presented to the United Nations, June 2015.

Mantymaki, Tina, 'Women who Kill Men: Gender, Agency and Subversion in Swedish Crime Novels', *European Journal of Women's Studies*, 20/4 (2013), 441–54.

Marcal, Katrine, *Who Cooked Adam Smith's Dinner?* (London, Portobello Books, 2015).

Marcuse, Herbert, *Eros and Civilisation: Studies in the Ideology of Advanced Industrial Societies* (London and New York, Routledge, 1964).

Marx, Karl, *Capital. Vol. 1* (London, Lawrence and Wishart, 1970).

Marx, Karl, 'The Eighteenth Brumaire of Louis Bonaparte', in Karl Marx and Frederick Engels, *Selected Works. Vol. 1* (London, Lawrence and Wishart, 1958), 247–344.

Marx, Karl and Frederick Engels, *The Holy Family, or Critique of Critical Criticism* (Moscow, Progress, 1975).

Maxton, Graeme, 'Economic Growth Doesn't Create Jobs, It Destroys Them', *Guardian*, 21 April 2016, http://www.theguardian.com/sustainable-business/2015/apr/21/jobs-economic-growth-inequality-environment-club-of-rome.

McDowell, Linda, *Capital Culture: Gender at Work in the City* (Oxford and Malden, MA, Blackwell, 1997).

McKenzie, Lisa, *Getting By: Estates, Class and Culture in Austerity Britain* (Bristol, Policy Press, 2014).

Melby, Kari, Anna-Birte Ravn and Christina Carlsson Wetterberg, *Gender Equality and Welfare Politics in Scandinavia: The Limits of Political Ambition?* (Bristol, Policy Press, 2009).

Merck, Mandy and Stella Sandford (eds.), *Further Adventures of the Dialectic of Sex* (London, Palgrave Macmillan, 2010).

Millett, Kate, *Sexual Politics* (New York, Doubleday, 1970).

Mills, C.W., *The Power Elite* (New York, Oxford University Press, 1959).

Mills, C.W., *White Collar* (New York, Oxford University Press, 1956).

Mishra, Pankaj, 'After the Paris Attacks: It's Time for a New Enlightenment', *Guardian*, 20 January 2015, http://www.theguardian. com/news/2015/jan/20/-sp-after-paris-its-time-for-new-enlighten ment.

Mitchell, Juliet, *Mad Men and Medusas: Reclaiming Hysteria* (London, Penguin, 2000).

Mitchell, Juliet, *The Selected Melanie Klein* (New York, Free Press, 1987).

Mkhize, Nandi, 'Violence Against Women: A Human Rights Issue at Home',10 December 2014, http://www.fawcettsociety.org.uk/blog/ violence-women-human-rights-issue-home.

Moi, Toril, *Simone de Beauvoir: The Making of an Intellectual Woman* (Oxford, Blackwell, 1994).

Moore, Charles, *Margaret Thatcher: The Authorised Biography. Vol. 1: Not for Turning* (London, Allen Lane, 2013).

Moore, Charles, *Margaret Thatcher: The Authorised Biography. Vol. 2: Everything She Wants* (London, Allen Lane, 2015).

Moore, Henrietta, *The Subject of Anthropology: Gender, Symbolism and Psychoanalysis* (Cambridge and Malden, MA, Polity, 2007).

Morrow, Colette and Terri Ann Frederick (eds.), *Getting In Is Not Enough* (Baltimore, Johns Hopkins University Press, 2012).

Mukherjee, Suroopa, *Surviving Bhopal: Dancing Bodies, Written Texts and Oral Testimonies of Women in the Wake of an Industrial Disaster* (London and New York, Palgrave Macmillan, 2010).

Mulholland, Hélène, 'David Willetts blames feminism over lack of jobs for working men', *Guardian*, 1 April 2011.

Munro, V., 'Sexual Autonomy', in M. Dubber and T. Hoernle (eds.) *The*

Oxford Handbook of Criminal Law (Oxford, Oxford University Press, 2014), 747–67.

Murfin, Ross, 'Novel Representations: Politics and Victorian Fiction', in Jerome J. McCann (ed.) *Victorian Connections* (Charlottesville, University Press of Virginia, 1989), 31–59.

Nicholson, Virginia, *Perfect Wives in Ideal Homes* (London, Penguin, 2015).

Nousiainen, L., A. Holli, J. Kantola, M. Saari and L. Hart, 'Theorising Gender Equality: Perspectives on Power and Legitimacy', *Social Politics*, 20/1 (2013), 41–64.

Nussbaum, Martha, *Political Emotion: Why Love Matters for Justice* (Cambridge, MA, Harvard University Press, 2013).

Oakley, Ann, *From Here to Maternity: Becoming a Mother* (London, Penguin, 1986).

Oakley, Ann, *Housewife* (London, Penguin, 1990).

Olivier Bell, Anne (ed.), *The Diary of Virginia Bell. Vol. One: 1915–1919* (London and New York, Harcourt Brace Jovanovich, 1977).

Orbach, Susie, *Fat Is a Feminist Issue* (London, Arrow, 2006).

Ortner, Sherry B., 'Is Female to Male as Nature is to Culture?', *Feminist Studies*, ,1/2 (1972), 5–31.

Parla, Ayse, '"The Honour" of the State: Virginity Examinations in Turkey', *Feminist Studies*, 27 (2001), 65–88.

Parpart, Jane and Kevin Partridge, 'Soldiering On: Pushing Militarized Masculinities into New Territory', in Mary Evans, Clare Hemmings, Marsha Henry, Hazel Johnstone, Sumi Madhok, Ania Plomien and Sadie Wearing (eds.) *The Sage Handbook of Feminist Theory* (LondonNew York, Sage, 2014), 550–65.

Pearson, Ruth and Diane Elson, 'Transcending the Impact of the Financial Crisis in the United Kingdom: Towards Plan F – A Feminist Economic Strategy', *Feminist Review*, 109 (2015), 8–30.

Penny, Laurie, *Cybersexism: Sex, Gender and Power on the Internet* (London, Bloomsbury, 2013).

Penny, Laurie, *Meat Market: Female Flesh under Capitalism* (London, Zero Books, 2011).

Penny, Laurie, *Unspeakable Things: Sex, Lies and Revolution* (London and New York, Bloomsbury, 2014).

Pickett, Kate and Richard Wilkinson, *The Spirit Level: Why Equality is Better for Everyone* (London, Penguin, 2010).

Piketty, Thomas, *Capital in the Twenty-First Century* (Cambridge, MA, Harvard University Press, 2013).

Plath, Sylvia, *The Bell Jar* (London, Faber and Faber, 1963).

Plomien, Ania (ed.), 'Economy', in Mary Evans, Clare Hemmings, Marsha Henry, Hazel Johnstone, Sumi Madhok, Ania Plomien and Sadie Wearing (eds.) *The Sage Handbook of Feminist Theory* (London and New York, Sage, 2014), 389-528.

Prendergast, Christopher, Letter to the *Guardian*, 5 February 2014, http://www.theguardian.com/politics/2014/feb/05/fantasies-shaping-childrens-futures.

Reay, Diane, 'Beyond Consciousness? The Psychic Language of Social Class', *Sociology*, Special Issue on Class, Culture and Identity, 39/5 (2005), 911–28.

Reich, Wilhelm, *The Mass Psychology of Fascism* (New York, Orgone Institution Press, 1946).

Reid, Margaret, 'The Economic Contribution of Homemakers', *Annals of the American Academy of Political and Social Science*, 251 (1947), 61–9.

Reid, Margaret, *The Economics of Household Production* (New York, John Wiley, and London, Chapman and Hall, 1934).

Rich, Adrienne, 'Compulsory Heterosexuality and Lesbian Experience', *Signs*, 5/4 (1980), 631–60.

Rofel, Lisa, *Desiring China: Experiments in Neoliberalism, Sexuality and Public Culture* (Durham, NC, Duke University Press, 2007).

Rosin, Hanna, *The End of Men: And the Rise of Women* (New York and London, Penguin, 2012).

Rose, Gillian, *Love's Work* (London, Chatto and Windus,1995).

Rose, Jacqueline, 'We Need a Bold, Scandalous Feminism', *Guardian*, 17 October 2014, p. 4.

Rose, Jacqueline, *Women in Dark Times* (London, Bloomsbury, 2014).

Rosenberg, Tracey, 'The Awkward Blot: George Eliot's Reception and the Ideal Woman Writer', *Nineteenth Century Gender Studies*, 3/1 (2007), 1–15.

Rude, George, *The Crowd in History: A Study of Popular Disturbances in France and England, 1730–1840* (New York, Wiley, 1964).

Sage, Lorna, *Bad Blood: A Memoir* (London, Fourth Estate, 2001).

Said, Edward, *Reflections on Exile and Other Literary and Cultural Essays* (London, Granta, 2001).

Samuel, Raphael, *Island Stories: Unravelling Britain* (London, Verso, 1998).

Samuel, Raphael, *Theatres of Memory* (London, Verso, 1994).

Sandberg, Sheryl, *Lean in: Women, Work and the Will to Lead* (New York, Alfred A. Knopf, 2013).

Savage, Mike, 'The "Class Ceiling" and the New Class War', *Guardian*, 22 October 2015.

Savage, Mike, *Social Class in the 21st Century* (London, Penguin, 2014).

Savage, Mike, Fiona Devine, Niall Cunningham, Mark Taylor, Yaojun Li, Johs Hjellbrekke, Brigitte Le Roux, Sam Friedman and Andrew Miles, 'A New Model of Social Class? Findings from the BBC's Great British Class Survey Experiment', *Sociology*, 47/2 (2013), 219–50.

Schilt, Kristen, *Just One of the Guys: Transgender Men and the Persistence of Gender Inequality* (Chicago, University of Chicago Press, 2010).

Schilt, Kristen and Lauren Westbrook, 'Doing Gender, Determining Gender', *Gender and Society*, 28/1 (2014), 440–64.

Scott, Joan Wallach, *The Fantasy of Feminist History* (Durham, NC, Duke University Press, 2011).

Seabrook, Jeremy, *Pauperland: Poverty and the Poor in Britain* (London, Hurst, 2013).

Segal, Lynne, *Is the Future Female?* (London, Virago, 1987).

Segal, Lynne, *Out of Time: The Pleasures and the Perils of Ageing* (London and New York, Verso, 2013).

Simmel, Georg, 'Spatial and Urban Culture', in David Frisby and Mike Featherstone (eds.) *Simmel on Culture: Selected Writings* (London, Sage, 1997), 137–85.

Slaughter, Anne-Marie, *Unfinished Business: Women, Men, Work, Family* (New York, Random House, 2015).

Smart, Barry (ed.), *Michel Foucault* (London and New York, Routledge, 1995).

Smith, Adam, *The Wealth of Nations*, first published 1776 (Harmondsworth, Penguin, 1970).

Spring Rice, Margery, *Working Class Wives: Their Health and Condition*, first published 1939 (London, Virago, 1981).

Stedman Jones, Daniel, *Masters of the Universe* (Princeton, NJ, and London, Princeton University Press, 2012).

Steedman, Carolyn, *Labours Lost: Domestic Service and the Making of Modern England* (Cambridge, Cambridge University Press, 2009).

Steedman, Carolyn, *Landscape for a Good Woman: A Story of Two Lives* (London, Virago, 1986).

Stevenson, Adlai, 'Speech at the Commencement Ceremony, Smith College 1955', http://coursesa.matrix.msu.edu/~hst306/documents/stevenson.html.

Stiglitz, Joseph, 'The Global Crisis, Social Protection and Jobs', *International Labour Review*, 152 (2013), 93–106.

Striking Women, 'Striking Out: The Grunwick Dispute', www.striking-women.org/module/striking-out/grunwick-dispute.

Stuckler, David and Basu Sanjay, *The Body Economic: Why Austerity Kills* (New York, Basic Books, 2013).

Taylor, Barbara, *Eve and the New Jerusalem: Socialism and Feminism in the Nineteenth Century* (London, Virago, 1983).

Taylor, Barbara, *The Last Asylum: A Memoir of Madness in our Times* (London and New York, Hamish Hamilton, 2014).

Tilly, Louise A. and Joan W. Scott, *Women, Work and Family* (London and New York, Methuen, 1987).

Tirado, Linda, *Hand to Mouth: The Truth about Being Poor in a Wealthy World* (London, Virago, 2014).

Treacher Kabesh, Amal, *Postcolonial Masculinities: Emotions, Histories and Ethics* (Farnham and Burlington, VT, Ashgate, 2013).

Tyler, Imogen, *Revolting Subjects: Social Abjection and Resistance in Neoliberal Britain* (London, Zed Books, 2013).

UN, 'Facts and Figures: Ending Violence against Women', http://www.unwomen.org/en/what-we-do/ending-violence-against-women/facts-and-figures.

Varoufakis, Y., 'Egalitarianism's Latest Foe: A Critical Review of Thomas Piketty's *Capital in the 21st Century*', *Real World Economics*, Special Issue on Piketty's *Capital*, October (2014), 18–35.

Walters, Margaret, 'The Rights and Wrongs of Women: Harriet Martineau, Mary Wollstonecraft and Simone de Beauvoir', in Ann Oakley and Juliet Mitchell (eds.) *The Rights and Wrongs of Women* (Harmondsworth, Penguin, 1976), 305–78.

War on Want, 'Never Again: Making Fashion's Factories Safe', April 2014, www.waronwant.org/resources/never-again-making-fashions-factories-safe

Wattis, Louise and Liz James, 'Exploring Order and Disorder', *European Journal of Women's Studies*, 20/3 (2013), 264–78.

Weber, Max, *From Max Weber: Essays in Sociology* (London, Routledge and Kegan Paul, 1964).

Weber, Max, *The Protestant Ethic and the Spirit of Capitalism* (New York, Charles Scribner & Sons,1958).

Weeks, Jeffrey, *Sex, Politics and Society: The Regulation of Sexuality since 1800*, 3rd edn (London, Routledge, 2012).

Weeks, Jeffrey, *The World We Have Won* (London and New York, Routledge, 2007).

Wells, C., 'The Impact of Feminist Thinking on Criminal Law and Justice: Contradiction, Complexity, Conviction and Connection', *Criminal Law Review*, 4 (2004), 503–15.

Williams, Zoe, *Get it Together: Why We Need Better Politics* (London, Hutchinson, 2015).

Wilson, Amrit, *Finding a Voice: Asian Women in Britain* (London, Virago, 1978).

Wilson, Elizabeth, *Adorned in Dreams: Fashion and Modernity*, rev. edn (London and New York, I.B. Tauris, 2007).

Wilson, Kalpana, ' "Race", Gender and Neoliberalism: Changing Visual Representations in Development', *Third World Quarterly*, 32/2 (2011), 315–31.

Wittig, Monique, *Les Guérillères*, first published 1969 (English translation: London, Peter Owen, 1971).

Wittig, Monique, *The Straight Mind and Other Essays* (Boston, Beacon Press, 1992).

Wolf, Alison, *The XX Factor: How Working Women Are Creating a New Society* (London, Profile, 2013).

Wollstonecraft, Mary, *A Vindication of the Rights of Woman* (London, 1792).

Yamamori, Toru, 'A Feminist Way to Unconditional Basic Income: Claimants Unions and Women's Liberation Movements in the 1970s', *Basic Income Studies*, 9/1–2 (2014), 1–24.

Yates, Richard, *Revolutionary Road* (New York, Little, Brown, 1961).

Yörük, Erdem and Murat Yüksel, 'Turkey's Hot Summer', *New Left Review*, 89 (2014), 103–23.

Index